Microsoft® PowerPoint® 2002

10

MINUTE

GUIDE

201 West 103rd Street
Indianapolis, IN 46290

Joe Habraken

Ten Minute Guide to Microsoft® PowerPoint® 2002 ©2002 by Que® Corporation

International Standard Book Number: 0-7897-2637-8

Library of Congress Catalog Card Number: 2001090294

Printed in the United States of America

First Printing: November, 2001

04 03 02   8 7 6 5

Trademarks

Warning and Disclaimer

Associate Publisher
Greg Wiegand

Acquisitions Editor
Stephanie J. McComb

Managing Editor
Thomas Hayes

Project Editor
Tonya Simpson

Indexer
Ken Johnson

Proofreader
Melissa Lynch

Technical Editor
Dallas Releford

Team Coordinator
Sharry Gregory

Interior Designer
Gary Adair

Cover Designer
Sandra Schroeder

Page Layout
Gloria Schurick

Contents at a Glance

TABLE OF CONTENTS

Dedication

*To all of humanity, in the hopes that a time will come when we realize
world peace, love, and understanding.*

Acknowledgments

Creating books like this takes a real team effort. I would like to thank
Stephanie McComb, our acquisitions editor, who worked very hard to
assemble the team that made this book a reality. Also a tip of the hat
and a thanks to Dallas Releford, who as the technical editor for the
project did a fantastic job making sure that everything was correct and
suggested a number of additions that made the book even more techni-
cally sound. Finally, a great big thanks to our project editor, Tonya
Simpson, who ran the last leg of the race and made sure the book
made it to press on time—what a great team of professionals!

TELL US WHAT YOU THINK!

As the reader of this book, *you* are our most important critic and commentator. We value your opinion and want to know what we're doing right, what we could do better, what areas you'd like to see us publish in, and any other words of wisdom you're willing to pass our way.

As an associate publisher for Que, I welcome your comments. You can fax, email, or write me directly to let me know what you did or didn't like about this book—as well as what we can do to make our books stronger.

Please note that I cannot help you with technical problems related to the topic of this book, and that due to the high volume of mail I receive, I might not be able to reply to every message.

When you write, please be sure to include this book's title and author as well as your name and phone or fax number. I will carefully review your comments and share them with the author and editors who worked on the book.

Fax: 317-581-4666

E-mail: feedback@quepublishing.com

Mail: Greg Wiegand
          Que
          201 West 103rd Street
          Indianapolis, IN 46290 USA

Introduction

Microsoft PowerPoint 2002 is a powerful presentation software application that provides an easy-to-use interface and all the tools you need to build personal and business presentations. You have the option to create your presentations from scratch or to use the AutoContent Wizard and design templates that help you build a variety of different presentation types.

THE WHAT AND WHY OF MICROSOFT POWERPOINT

Microsoft PowerPoint not only enables you to create your own presentations; it also provides features and tools that enable you to easily enhance the slides in your presentation and rearrange the slides as needed. You will be able to quickly create exciting presentations using the following features:

- The AutoContent Wizard walks you through each step of creating a new presentation and supplies dummy text that you can replace with your own information.

- Views such as the Outline view and the Slide Sorter make it easy to arrange your presentation slides in a logical order.

- Design templates enable you to add color, background patterns, and special fonts to the slides in your presentation.

- Animation schemes can be used to add transitions as you move from slide to slide that add visual impact to your presentation.

- You can add clip art to your slides to provide visual interest. The Clipart library also includes motion clips and sounds.

While providing you with many complex features, Microsoft PowerPoint is easy to learn. It enables you to build presentations that can be shown on a computer, printed, or saved in a format so that the presentation can be viewed on the World Wide Web. This book will help you understand the possibilities awaiting you with Microsoft PowerPoint 2002.

WHY QUE'S *10 MINUTE GUIDE TO MICROSOFT POWERPOINT 2002*?

The *10 Minute Guide to Microsoft PowerPoint 2002* can save you precious time while you get to know the different features provided by Microsoft PowerPoint. Each lesson is designed to be completed in 10 minutes or less, so you'll be up to snuff on basic and advanced PowerPoint features and skills quickly.

Although you can jump around among lessons, starting at the beginning is a good plan. The bare-bones basics are covered first, and more advanced topics are covered later. Following the lessons sequentially will allow you to walk through all the steps of creating and enhancing personal and business presentations.

INSTALLING POWERPOINT

You can install Microsoft PowerPoint 2002 on a computer running Microsoft Windows 98, Windows NT 4.0, Windows 2000, and Windows XP. Microsoft PowerPoint can be purchased as a standalone product on its own CD-ROM, or it can be purchased as part of the Microsoft Office XP suite (which comes on several CD-ROMs). Whether you are installing PowerPoint as a standalone product or as part of the Microsoft Office XP suite, the installation steps are basically the same.

To install PowerPoint, follow these steps:

1. Start your computer, and then insert the PowerPoint or Microsoft XP Office CD in the CD-ROM drive. The CD-ROM should autostart, showing you the opening installation screen (for either PowerPoint or Office, depending on the CD you are working with).

2. If the CD-ROM does not autostart, choose **Start**, **Run**. In the Run dialog box, type the letter of the CD-ROM drive, followed by `setup` (for example, `d:\setup`). If necessary, click the **Browse** button to locate and select the CD-ROM drive and the setup.exe program.

3. When the Setup Wizard prompts you, enter your name, organization, and CD key in the appropriate box.

4. Choose **Next** to continue.

5. The next wizard screen provides instructions to finish the installation. Complete the installation, and select **Next** to advance from screen to screen after providing the appropriate information requested by the wizard.

After you complete the installation from the CD, icons for PowerPoint and any other Office applications you have installed will be provided on the Windows Start menu. Lesson 2 in this book provides you with a step-by-step guide to starting PowerPoint 2002.

CONVENTIONS USED IN THIS BOOK

To help you move through the lessons easily, these conventions are used:

On-screen text	On-screen text appears in bold type.
`Text you should type`	Information you need to type appears in bold monospaced type.
Items you select	Commands, options, and icons you should select and keys you should press appear in bold type.

In telling you to choose menu commands, this book uses the format *menu title*, *menu command*. For example, the statement "Choose **File**, **Properties**" means to open the File menu and select the Properties command.

In addition to those conventions, the *10 Minute Guide to Microsoft PowerPoint 2002* uses the following icons to identify helpful information:

PLAIN ENGLISH

Plain English   New or unfamiliar terms are defined in term sidebars.

TIP

Tips   Read these tips for ideas that cut corners and confusion.

CAUTION

Cautions   Cautions identify areas where new users often run into trouble; these tips offer practical solutions to those problems.

LESSON 1
What's New in PowerPoint 2002?

In this lesson, you are introduced to PowerPoint's powerful presentation features, and you learn what's new in PowerPoint 2002.

GETTING THE MOST OUT OF POWERPOINT 2002

PowerPoint is a powerful presentation application that enables you to create presentations that can be viewed on a computer. Using PowerPoint, you can print handouts or create film slides for a presentation. PowerPoint also enables you to add animation and sound to your presentations, which makes it the perfect presentation tool for business presentations or classroom lectures.

PowerPoint provides several features to help you create personal and business presentations. These features range from the AutoContent Wizard and design templates, which help you create slides for your presentation, to tools such as the Outline and Slide Sorter views, which make it easy for you to rearrange the slides in your presentation. You can add images, sounds, and many different types of objects to your slides as you create informative and visually interesting presentations.

Whether you are new to PowerPoint or are familiar with previous versions of PowerPoint, this book will walk you through the basics of creating a new presentation in PowerPoint 2002 and look at several different ways to enhance your PowerPoint slides. You can even save your PowerPoint presentations in HTML format so they can be viewed on the World Wide Web.

NEW FEATURES IN POWERPOINT 2002

PowerPoint 2002 embraces a number of features that were first introduced with the release of PowerPoint 2000. For example, PowerPoint
2002 uses the same adaptive menu and toolbar system found in
PowerPoint 2000 that customizes the commands and icons listed
based on the commands you use most frequently.

PowerPoint 2002 also builds on the features found in the previous version of PowerPoint by offering many new features that make it easier
for you to create, arrange, and format the slides in your presentation.
New features in PowerPoint 2002 range from the different views that
you can use to display your presentation, to voice dictation, to new
ways to quickly get help.

For example, you will find that getting help in PowerPoint 2002 is
even easier than in previous versions of PowerPoint. A new feature,
the Ask a Question Box, has been added to the top left of the
PowerPoint application window, making it easier for you to get help
on a particular topic as you work. The various ways to get help in
PowerPoint are covered in Lesson 10, "Getting Help in Microsoft
PowerPoint." Let's take a survey of some of the other new features
that are provided by PowerPoint 2002.

INTRODUCING TASK PANES

One of the biggest changes to the PowerPoint environment (and all the
Microsoft Office XP member applications, such as Word 2002, Excel
2002, and Access 2002) is the introduction of the Office task pane.
The task pane is a special pane that appears on the right side of the
PowerPoint application window. It is used to provide access to many
PowerPoint features that formerly were controlled using dialog boxes.

For example, when you want to add slides to a presentation or change
the layout of a slide already in the presentation, you will use the Slide
Layout task pane. This task pane appears in Figure 1.1. Creating new
slides is discussed in Lesson 6, "Inserting, Deleting, and Copying
Slides."

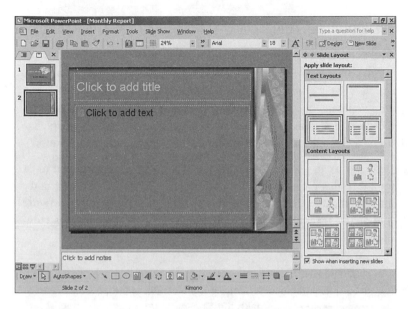

FIGURE 1.1
The Slide Layout task pane enables you to select the layout for the current slide.

Other task panes that you will run across as you use PowerPoint are the Slide Design task pane, the Office Clipboard, and the Clip Gallery. The Slide Design task pane enables you to select the design template for the presentation and the color or animation scheme used on a particular slide (this task pane is discussed in Lesson 5, "Changing a Presentation's Look").

The Office Clipboard enables you to copy or cut multiple items from a slide and then paste them onto an existing or new slide. The Clip Gallery enables you to insert clip art, sounds, and animated content onto your slides. Task panes are discussed throughout this book as you explore the various PowerPoint features.

INTRODUCING VOICE DICTATION AND VOICE COMMANDS

One of the most exciting new features in PowerPoint 2002 (and the entire Office XP suite) is voice dictation and voice-activated commands. If your computer is outfitted with a sound card, speakers, and a microphone (or a microphone with an earphone headset), you can dictate information into your PowerPoint presentations. You also can use voice commands to activate the menu system in that application.

Before you can really take advantage of the Speech feature, you must train it so that it can more easily recognize your speech patterns and intonation. After the Speech feature is trained, you can effectively use it to dictate text entries or access various application commands without a keyboard or mouse.

 CAUTION

> **Requirements for Getting the Most Out of the Speech Feature**   To make the Speech feature useful, you will need a fairly high-quality microphone. Microsoft suggests a microphone/headset combination. The Speech feature also requires a more powerful computer. Microsoft suggests using a computer with 128MB of RAM and a Pentium II (or later) processor running at a minimum of 400MHz. A computer that meets or exceeds these higher standards should be capable of getting the most out of the Speech feature.

You might want to explore the other lessons in this book if you are new to PowerPoint before you attempt to use the Speech feature. Having a good understanding of how PowerPoint operates and the features that it provides will allow you to get the most out of the Speech feature.

TRAINING THE SPEECH FEATURE

The first time you start the Speech feature in PowerPoint, you are required to configure and train it. Follow these steps to get the Speech feature up and running:

1. In PowerPoint, select the **Tools** menu and select **Speech**. The Welcome to Office Speech Recognition dialog box appears. To begin the process of setting up your microphone and training the Speech feature, click the **Next** button.

2. The first screen of the Microphone Wizard appears. It asks you to be sure that your microphone and speakers are connected to your computer. If you have a headset microphone, this screen shows you how to adjust the microphone for use. Click **Next** to continue.

3. The next wizard screen asks you to read a short text passage so that your microphone volume level can be adjusted (see Figure 1.2). When you have finished reading the text, click **Next** to continue.

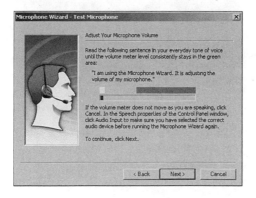

FIGURE 1.2
The Microphone Wizard adjusts the volume of your microphone.

4. On the next screen, you are told that if you have a headset microphone, you can click **Finish** and proceed to the speech recognition training. If you have a different type of microphone, you are asked to read another text passage. The text then is played back to you to determine whether the microphone is placed at an appropriate distance from your mouth. When you get a satisfactory playback, click **Finish**.

When you finish working with the Microphone Wizard, the Voice Training Wizard appears. This wizard collects samples of your speech and, in essence, educates the Speech feature as to how you speak.

To complete the voice training process, follow these steps:

1. After reading the information on the opening screen, click **Next** to begin the voice training process.

2. On the next screen, you are asked to provide your gender and age (see Figure 1.3). After specifying the correct information, click **Next**.

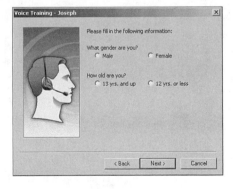

FIGURE 1.3
Supply the voice trainer with your gender and age.

3. The next wizard screen provides an overview of how the voice training will proceed. You also are provided with directions for how to pause the training session. Click **Next**.

4. The next wizard screen reminds you to adjust your microphone. You also are reminded that you need a quiet room when training the Speech feature. When you are ready to begin training the speech recognition feature, click **Next**.

5. On the next screen, you are asked to read some text. As the wizard recognizes each word, the word is highlighted. After finishing with this screen, continue by clicking **Next**.

6. You are asked to read text on several subsequent screens. Words are selected as the wizard recognizes them.

7. Your profile is updated when you complete the training screens. Click **Finish** on the wizard's final screen.

You are now ready to use the Speech feature. The next two sections discuss using the Voice Dictation and Voice Command features.

CAUTION

The Speech Feature Works Better Over Time Be advised that the voice feature's performance improves as you use it. As you learn to pronounce your words more carefully, the Speech feature tunes itself to your speech patterns. You might need to do additional training sessions to fine-tune the Speech feature.

USING VOICE DICTATION

When you are ready to start dictating text into a PowerPoint slide, put on your headset microphone or place your standalone microphone in the proper position that you determined when you used the Microphone Wizard. When you're ready to go, select the **Tools** menu, and then select **Speech**. The Language bar appears, as shown in Figure 1.4. If necessary, click the **Dictation** button on the toolbar (if the Dictation button is not already activated or depressed).

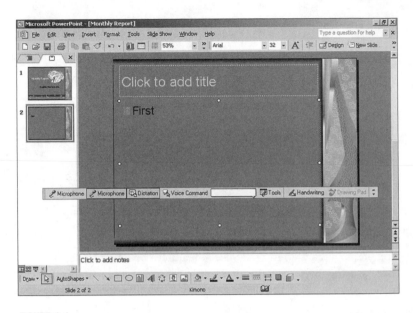

FIGURE 1.4
Dictating text into a PowerPoint slide.

After you enable the Dictation button, you can begin dictating your
text. Figure 1.4 shows text being dictated into a PowerPoint slide.
When you want to put a line break into the text, say "New line." You
can place punctuation in the document by saying the name of a particular punctuation mark, such as "period" or "comma."

CAUTION

**How Do I Insert the Word "Comma" Rather Than the
Punctuation Mark?**   Because certain keywords, such as
"period" or "comma," are used to insert punctuation
during dictation, you must spell these words out if you
want to include them in the text. To do this, say
"spelling mode," and then spell out the word, such as c-
o-m-m-a. As soon as you dictate an entire word, the
spelling mode is ended.

When you have finished dictating into the document, click the **Microphone** button on the Language bar (the second Microphone button from the left; the first is used to select the current speech driver, which you can leave as the default). When you click the **Microphone** button, the Language bar collapses, hiding the **Dictation** and the **Voice Command** buttons. You also can stop Dictation mode by saying "microphone."

You can minimize the Language bar by clicking the **Minimize** button on the right end of the bar. This sends the Language bar to the Windows System Tray (it appears as a small square icon marked EN, if you are using the English version of Office).

With the Language bar minimized in the System Tray, you can quickly open it when you need it. Click the **Language Bar** icon in the System Tray, and then select **Show the Language Bar** (which is the only choice provided when you click on the Language Bar icon).

Using the Dictation feature correctly requires that you know how to get the Speech feature to place the correct text or characters into PowerPoint. For more help with the dictation feature, consult the Microsoft PowerPoint Help system (discussed in Lesson 10).

USING VOICE COMMANDS

Another tool the Speech feature provides is voice commands. You can open and select menus in an application, and even navigate dialog boxes, using voice commands.

To use voice commands, open the Language bar (click **Tools**, **Speech**). Click the **Microphone** icon, if necessary, to expand the Language bar. Then, click the **Voice Command** icon on the bar (or say "voice command").

To open a particular menu, such as the Format menu, say "format." Then, to open a particular submenu, such as Font, say "font." In the case of these voice commands, the Font dialog box opens.

You then can navigate a particular dialog box using voice commands. In the Font dialog box, for example, to change the size of the font, say "size"; this activates the Size box that controls font size. Then, say the size of the font, such as "14." You can activate other font attributes in the dialog box in this manner. Say the name of the area of the dialog box you want to use, and then say the name of the feature you want to turn on or select.

When you have finished working with a particular dialog box, say "OK" (or "Cancel" or "Apply," as needed), and the dialog box closes and provides you with the features you selected in the dialog box. When you have finished using voice commands, say "microphone," or click the **Microphone** icon on the Language bar.

Believe it or not, you also can activate buttons on the various toolbars using voice commands. For example, you could turn on bold by saying "bold." The Bold button on the Formatting toolbar becomes active. To turn bold off, say "bold" again.

In this lesson, you were introduced to PowerPoint 2002 and some of the new features available in this latest version of Microsoft PowerPoint, such as task panes and the Speech feature. In the next lesson, you learn how to start PowerPoint and work in the application window.

LESSON 2
Working in PowerPoint

In this lesson, you learn how to start and exit PowerPoint. You also learn about the PowerPoint presentation window.

STARTING POWERPOINT

PowerPoint provides a complete environment for creating, managing, and viewing presentation slides. To start PowerPoint, follow these steps:

1. Click the **Start** button.

2. Move your mouse pointer to **Programs**. A menu of programs appears.

3. Move your mouse pointer to the **Microsoft PowerPoint** icon and click it. The PowerPoint application window opens, as shown in Figure 2.1.

Outline and Slides pane   Slide pane   Notes pane   Task pane

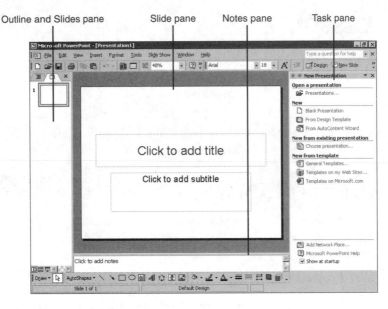

FIGURE 2.1
The PowerPoint window is divided into several panes.

The first thing you see when you open PowerPoint is that the application window is divided into different areas. The default view for PowerPoint is the Normal view (you learn about the different PowerPoint views in Lesson 4, "Working with Slides in Different Views"). On the left of the screen is a pane that can be used to switch between an Outline and Slides view of the current presentation. In the center of the PowerPoint application window is the Slide pane; this is where you work individually on each slide in the presentation.

Below the Slide pane is the Notes pane, which enables you to add notes to the presentation for each slide. On the far right of the application window is the New Presentation task pane. The task pane provides different commands and features depending on what you are currently doing in PowerPoint.

Getting Comfortable with the PowerPoint Window

Although PowerPoint looks a little different from the other Office applications, such as Word and Excel, all the standard Office application components, such as the menu bar and various toolbars, are available to you as you design your presentations. The basic element of a presentation is a slide, to which you add text and other objects, such as images, using the Slide pane (which is discussed in the next lesson). PowerPoint provides several slide layouts; each layout provides the necessary text boxes or clip-art boxes for creating a particular type of slide.

Adding text to a slide is very straightforward. Each slide that you add to a presentation (Lesson 6, "Inserting, Deleting, and Copying Slides," discusses inserting slides into a presentation) contains placeholder text that tells you what to type into a particular text box on the slide. For example, Figure 2.2 shows a title slide. Note that the top text box on the slide says Click to Add Title.

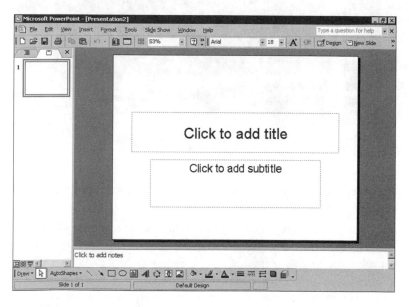

FIGURE 2.2
Click the placeholder text to input text into a slide.

To replace the placeholder text with your own text, just click the placeholder text. Then, you can type your entry into that text box.

Because a presentation consists of several slides, PowerPoint provides a thumbnail view of each slide in the presentation to the left of the Slides pane. Figure 2.3 shows an example of a complete presentation with a series of these thumbnail slides. This view can be used to keep track of your slides as you add them to the presentation and can even be used to rearrange slides in the presentation.

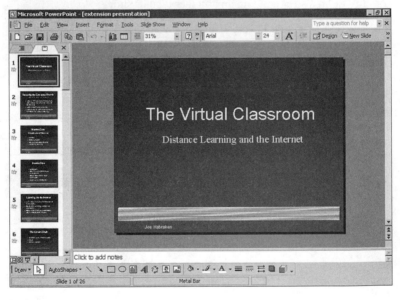

FIGURE 2.3
The Slides pane enables you to view thumbnails of the slides in the presentation.

Because presentations require a certain logical arrangement of information, you can view the slides in the presentation as an outline. This enables you to make sure that you have the facts presented by each slide in the proper order for the presentation. The Outline pane also enables you to move topics within the presentation and even move information from slide to slide. Figure 2.4 shows the Outline pane for a presentation that contains several slides.

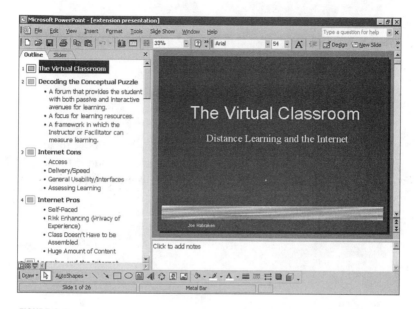

FIGURE 2.4
The Outline pane enables you to view the topic of each slide and each piece of text information included in a slide.

You learn about using the Slides and Outline pane in Lesson 4, "Working with Slides in Different Views." Lesson 4 shows you how you can edit the presentation's text in either the Outline or the Slide pane. Changes in one pane are reflected in the other pane. When you want to place a nontext object on a slide (such as a graphic), you do so in the Slide pane.

EXITING POWERPOINT

When you finish using PowerPoint, you can exit the application. This closes any open presentations (PowerPoint might prompt you to save changes to those presentations).

To exit PowerPoint, perform one of the following:

- Click the PowerPoint window's **Close** (X) button.

- Double-click the **Control Menu** icon in the left corner of the title bar, or click it once to open the **Control** menu and then select **Close**.

- Open the **File** menu and select **Exit**.

- Press **Alt+F4**.

In this lesson, you learned how to start and exit PowerPoint. In addition, you learned about the PowerPoint application window. In the next lesson, you learn how to create a new presentation.

LESSON 3
Creating a New Presentation

In this lesson, you learn several ways to create a presentation. You also learn how to save, close, and open an existing presentation.

THREE CHOICES FOR STARTING A NEW PRESENTATION

PowerPoint offers several ways to create a new presentation. Before you begin, decide which method is right for you:

- The AutoContent Wizard offers the highest degree of help. It walks you through each step of creating the new presentation. When you're finished, you have a standardized group of slides, all with a similar look and feel, for a particular situation. Each slide created includes dummy text that you can replace with your own text.

- A design template provides a professionally designed color, background, and font scheme that applies to the slides you create yourself. It does not provide sample slides.

- You can start from scratch and create a totally blank presentation. The means that you build the presentation from the ground up and create each slide in the presentation (beginners might want to use the wizard or templates until they get a feel for the overall design approach used to create a cohesive slide presentation).

PLAIN ENGLISH

Design Template   A design template is a preformatted presentation file (without any slides in it). When you select a template, PowerPoint applies the color scheme and general layout of the template to each slide you create for the presentation.

CREATING A NEW PRESENTATION WITH THE AUTOCONTENT WIZARD

With the AutoContent Wizard, you select the type of presentation you want to create (such as corporate, sales, or various projects), and PowerPoint creates an outline for the presentation.

The following steps describe how you use the AutoContent Wizard:

1. Select the **File** menu and select **New**. The New Presentation task pane appears on the right of the PowerPoint window, as shown in Figure 3.1 (if the Presentation task pane was already open in the window, you can skip to step 2).

FIGURE 3.1
Start the AutoContent Wizard from the task pane.

2. Click the **From AutoContent Wizard** link on the task pane.

3. The AutoContent Wizard starts. The opening wizard screen summarizes the process you should follow to create a new presentation. Click **Next** to continue.

4. The wizard provides you with category buttons for different categories of presentations: General, Corporate, Projects, Sales/Marketing, and Carnegie Coach. Select a category by

selecting the appropriate button (see Figure 3.2). To see all
the presentations available, click the **All** button.

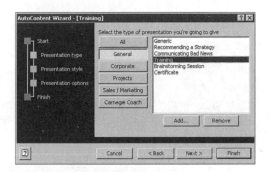

FIGURE 3.2
Select a category button to view a list of presentation types.

PLAIN ENGLISH

What Is the Carnegie Coach?   The Carnegie Coach provides presentations that can be used to sell your ideas
or motivate a team; they are named after Dale Carnegie,
the motivational speaker and author.

5. After selecting a particular category of presentations, select a
   presentation type in the list provided, and click **Next** to
   continue.

6. On the next screen, you select how you will give the presentation. Select one of the following options:

   • **Onscreen Presentation** — Choose this if you plan to
     use a computer and your PowerPoint file to present the
     show.

   • **Web Presentation**—Choose this if you are planning to
     distribute the presentation as a self-running or user-
     interactive show.

- **Black-and-White Overheads**—Choose this if you plan to make black-and-white transparencies for your show.

- **Color Overheads**—Choose this if you plan to make color transparencies for your show.

- **35mm Slides**—Choose this if you plan to send your PowerPoint presentation to a service bureau to have 35mm slides made. (You probably don't have such expensive and specialized equipment in your own company.)

7. After selecting how you will give the presentation, click **Next** to continue.

8. On the next screen, type the presentation title into the text box provided (see Figure 3.3). If you want to add a footer (such as your name) that will appear at the bottom of each slide of the presentation, click in the Footer box and type the appropriate text. If you do not want a date and/or slide number on each slide, deselect the **Date Last Updated** and/or **Slide Number** check boxes.

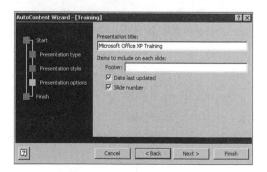

FIGURE 3.3
Provide a title for the presentation.

9. After supplying the presentation title and any optional information, click **Next** to continue.

10. PowerPoint takes you to the last wizard screen, where you should simply click **Finish**.

The title slide of your new presentation appears in the Slide pane. The entire presentation, including the dummy text placed on each slide, appears in the Outline pane on the left of the PowerPoint window (see Figure 3.4).

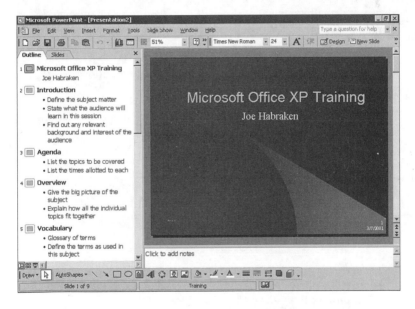

FIGURE 3.4
Your new presentation appears in the PowerPoint window.

You can start working on your presentation right away by replacing the dummy text on the slides with your own text. Just select the existing text in a text box and type right over it. You learn about editing text in slide text boxes in Lesson 8, "Adding and Modifying Slide Text."

CREATING A NEW PRESENTATION WITH A DESIGN TEMPLATE

A template is the middle ground between maximum hand-holding (the AutoContent Wizard) and no help at all (Blank Presentation). Two kinds of templates are available: presentation templates and design templates.

When you use the AutoContent Wizard, you use a presentation template. It contains not only formatting, but also sample slides that contain placeholder text. The other kind of template is a design template. It contains the overall formatting for the slides of the presentation but does not actually create any slides. If you want to use a presentation template, use the AutoContent Wizard, as explained in the preceding section.

To start a new presentation using a design template, follow these steps:

1. Select the **File** menu and select **New**. The New Presentation task pane appears on the right of the PowerPoint window.

 TIP

> **Select Your Task Pane**   If the task pane is already open for another PowerPoint feature, click the drop-down arrow on its title bar and select **New Presentation** from the list that appears.

2. On the New Presentation task pane, click the **From Design Template** link. PowerPoint switches to the Slide Design side pane, which displays a list of design templates, as shown in Figure 3.5. A blank title slide for the presentation appears in the Slide pane.

FIGURE 3.5
Design templates are listed in the task pane.

3. Click a template from the Available for Use section of the task pane. PowerPoint then formats the title slide in the Slide pane using the selected template.

You can select different templates to determine the best look for your presentation. When you have found the design template that you want to use, you can immediately start working on the slides for the presentation.

PLAIN ENGLISH

The Next Step?   Add more slides by clicking the **New Slide** button on the toolbar. Inserting slides into a presentation is covered in Lesson 6, "Inserting, Deleting, and Copying Slides."

CREATING A BLANK PRESENTATION

Your third option for creating a new presentation is to create a blank presentation. This means that you have to create all the slides from scratch. You then can select a design for the slides using the Slide Design task pane. You open this task pane by selecting **Format**, **Slide Design**. In the Slide Design task pane, be sure that the **Design Templates** icon is selected.

 Creating a new, blank presentation takes only a click: Click the **New** button on the Standard toolbar or click the **Blank Presentation** link on the New Presentation task pane. The new presentation appears in the PowerPoint window. A blank title slide is ready for you to edit.

SAVING A PRESENTATION

After you create a new presentation, it makes sense to save it. To save a presentation for the first time, follow these steps:

 1. Select **File**, **Save**, or just click the **Save** button on the Standard toolbar. The Save As dialog box appears (see Figure 3.6).

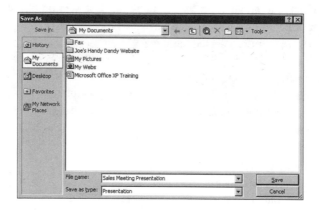

FIGURE 3.6
Type a name for your presentation into the Save As dialog box.

2. In the **File Name** text box, type the name you want to assign to the presentation. Your filenames can be as long as 255 characters and can include spaces.

3. The Save In box shows in which folder the file will be saved. The default is My Documents. To select a different drive location for the file, click the Save In drop-down arrow and select one from the list that appears. To save to a specific folder in the drive location you've selected, double-click the folder in which you want to store the file.

4. Click **Save**.

Now that you have named the file and saved it to a disk, you can save any changes you make simply by pressing **Ctrl+S** or clicking the **Save** button on the Standard toolbar. Your data is saved under the filename you assigned the presentation in the Save As dialog box.

To create a copy of a presentation under a different filename or location, select **File, Save As**. The Save As dialog box reappears; follow steps 2 to 4 as discussed in this section to give the file a new name or location.

CLOSING A PRESENTATION

You can close a presentation at any time. Note that although this closes the presentation window, it does not exit PowerPoint as with the methods discussed in Lesson 1. To close a presentation, follow these steps:

1. If more than one presentation is open, click a presentation's button on the Windows taskbar to make it the active presentation, or select the **Window** menu and select the presentation from the list provided.

2. Select **File** and then select **Close**, or click the presentation's **Close** (**x**) button. (It's the lower of the two Close buttons; the upper one is for the PowerPoint window.) If you haven't saved the presentation or if you haven't saved since you last made changes, a dialog box appears, asking whether you want to save.

3. To save your changes, click **Yes**. If this is a new presentation that has never been saved, refer to the steps in the preceding section for saving a presentation. If you have saved the file previously, the presentation window closes.

OPENING A PRESENTATION

Because a presentation, like Rome, is not built in a day, you probably will fine-tune a presentation over time. To open a saved presentation file that you want to work on, follow these steps:

1. Select **File**, **Open**, or click the **Open** button on the Standard toolbar. The Open dialog box appears (see Figure 3.7).

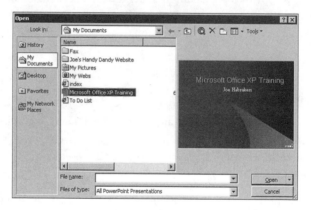

FIGURE 3.7
Select the presentation you want to open.

2. If the file isn't in the currently displayed folder, select the **Look In** drop-down arrow to choose from a list of other drives and/or folders.

3. Browse to the location containing the file, and double-click it to open it in PowerPoint.

FINDING A PRESENTATION FILE

If you're having trouble locating your file, PowerPoint can help you look. Follow these steps to find a file:

1. Select the **File** menu, and then select **Open** (if the Open dialog box is not already open).

2. Click the **Tools** drop-down button in the Open dialog box and select **Search**. The Search dialog box appears (see Figure 3.8).

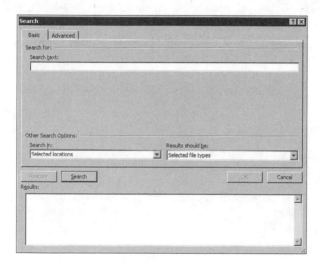

FIGURE 3.8
Use the Search dialog box to find a presentation on your computer.

3. In the **Search Text** box, type text that is contained in the presentation's filename. Use the Search In box to specify where you want the search to be conducted. In the Results Should Be box, specify the file types you want to be included in the search.

4. When you are ready to conduct the search, click the **Search** button.

5. Files that meet the search criteria are listed in the Results box (if you see your file in the Results box and the search is continuing, click the **Stop** button).

6. To open a file in the Results box, double-click the filename.

7. You are returned to the Open dialog box with the file listed in the File Name box. Click **OK** to open the file. A PowerPoint presentation then opens in the PowerPoint window.

In this lesson, you learned how to create a new presentation. You also learned how to save, close, open, and find presentations. In the next lesson, you learn how to work with slides in different views.

Lesson 4

Working with Slides in Different Views

In this lesson, you learn how to display a presentation in different views and how to edit slides in the Outline and Slide views.

Understanding PowerPoint's Different Views

PowerPoint can display your presentation in different views. Each of these views is designed for you to perform certain tasks as you create and edit a presentation. For example, Normal view has the Outline/Slides, Slide, and Notes panes; it provides an ideal environment for creating your presentation slides and to quickly view the organization of the slides or the information in the presentation (using the Outline or the Slides tabs). Another view, the Slide Sorter view, enables you to quickly rearrange the slides in the presentation (and is similar to the Slides view that shares the pane with the Outline tab when you are in the Normal view).

To change views, open the **View** menu and choose the desired view: **Normal**, **Slide Sorter**, **Slide Show**, or **Notes Page**.

- **Normal**—The default, three-pane view (which is discussed in Lesson 2, "Working in PowerPoint").

- **Slide Sorter**—This view shows all the slides as thumbnails so that you can easily rearrange them by dragging slides to new positions in the presentation (Figure 4.1 shows the Slide Sorter).

- **Slide Show**—A specialized view that enables you to preview and present your show onscreen. It enables you to test the presentation as you add slides, and it is used later when your presentation is complete.

- **Notes Page**—This view provides a large pane for creating notes for your speech. You also can type these notes in Normal view, but Notes Page view gives you more room and allows you to concentrate on your note text.

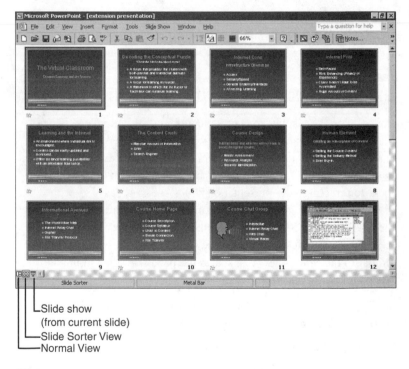

Slide show
(from current slide)
Slide Sorter View
Normal View

FIGURE 4.1
The Slide Sorter view is used to rearrange the slides in a presentation.

An even faster way to switch to certain views is to use the view buttons that are provided along the lower-left corner of the PowerPoint window. These buttons, from left to right, are Normal View, Slide Sorter View, and Slide Show (from current slide) button. A button is not provided for the Notes view.

MOVING FROM SLIDE TO SLIDE

PowerPoint provides several ways to move from slide to slide in the presentation. The particular view you are in somewhat controls the procedure for moving to a specific slide.

In the Normal view, you can move from slide to slide using these techniques:

- Click the **Outline** tab on the far left of the window. To go to a particular slide in the outline, click the slide icon next to the slide number (see Figure 4.2). The slide opens in the Slide pane.

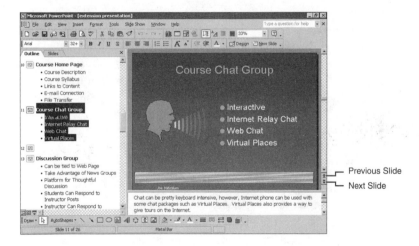

FIGURE 4.2
The Outline view can be used to quickly move to a particular slide.

- Press the **Page Up** or **Page Down** keys to move to the previous or next slide, respectively.

- Click the **Previous Slide** or **Next Slide** button just below the vertical scrollbar (refer to Figure 4.2), or drag the scroll box inside the vertical scrollbar until the desired slide number is displayed.

- Click the **Slides** tab on the far left of the PowerPoint window. This enables you to move from slide to slide in the Normal view by selecting a particular slide's thumbnail. When you click the thumbnail, the slide appears in the Slide pane.

You also can move from slide to slide in other views, such as the Slide Sorter view or the Slide Show view. In the Slide Sorter view (refer to Figure 4.1), just click a slide's thumbnail to move to that slide. You then can use any of the tools that PowerPoint provides to format the selected slide (or delete it). If you want to actually open a slide when you are working in the Slide Sorter view, so that you can edit the text it contains, double-click the slide. You are returned to the Normal view.

When you are actually showing a presentation in the Slide Show view, you can use the **Page Up** or **Page Down** keys to move from slide to slide (unless you have set up timers to change slides). You also can click a slide with the mouse to move to the next slide. You learn more about the Slide Show view in Lesson 16, "Presenting an Onscreen Slideshow."

INTRODUCTION TO INSERTING SLIDE TEXT

If you created a presentation in Lesson 3 using the AutoContent Wizard, you already have a presentation that contains several slides, but they won't contain the text you want to use. Slides created by the wizard contain placeholder text that you must replace. If you created a blank presentation or based a new presentation on a design template, you have only a title slide in that presentation, which, of course, needs to be personalized for your particular presentation. This means that additional slides will need to be added to the presentation. Lesson 6, "Inserting, Deleting, and Copying Slides," covers the creation of new slides for a presentation.

The sections that follow in this lesson look at the basics of inserting text into the text boxes provided on slides. You will look at adding new text boxes and formatting text in text boxes in Lesson 8, "Adding and Modifying Slide Text." Upcoming lessons also discuss how to add pictures and other objects to your PowerPoint slides.

PLAIN ENGLISH

> **Object**   An object is any item on a slide, including text, graphics, and charts.

EDITING TEXT IN THE SLIDE PANE

The text on your slides resides within boxes (all objects appear on a slide in their own boxes for easy manipulation). As shown in Figure 4.3, to edit text on a slide, click the text box to select it, and then click where you want the insertion point moved or select the text you want to replace.

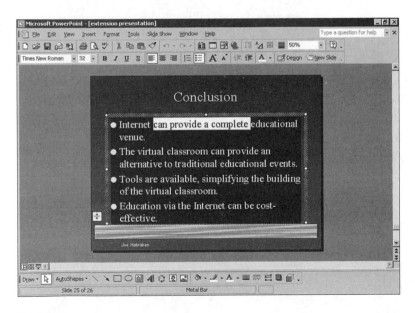

FIGURE 4.3
You can edit your text directly on the slide in the Slide pane.

When you work with the Slide pane, you might want to close the Outline/Slides pane. Just click the pane's **Close** button (**x**) to provide the Slide pane with the entire PowerPoint window (refer to Figure 4.3). In Lesson 8, "Adding and Modifying Slide Text," you'll learn more about adding text to a slide, including creating your own text boxes on a slide.

TIP

> **Opening the Outline Pane**   If you close the Outline pane to concentrate on the Slide pane, click **View**, **Normal (Restore Panes)** to restore it to the application window.

EDITING TEXT IN THE OUTLINE PANE

The Outline pane provides another way to edit text in a slide. To switch to the Outline view on the Outline/Slides pane, click the **Outline** tab. You simply click to move the insertion point where you want it (or select the range of text you want to replace) in the outline, and then type your text (see Figure 4.4). If you've placed the insertion point in the slide text (without selecting a range), press the **Del** key to delete characters to the right of the insertion point or press the **Backspace** key to delete characters to the left. If you've selected a range of text, either of these keys deletes the text. If you want to move the highlighted text, simply drag it to where you want it moved.

PLAIN ENGLISH

> **Larger Outline**   You might want to enlarge the Outline pane by dragging its divider to the right in the Normal view.

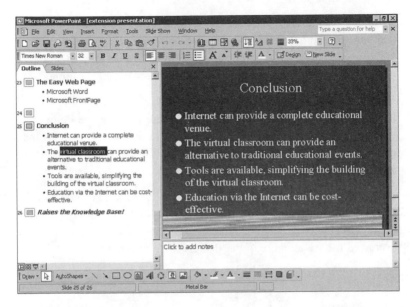

FIGURE 4.4
You can edit your text in Outline view.

TIP

> **Auto Word Select**   When you select text, PowerPoint
> selects whole words. If you want to select individual
> characters, open the **Tools** menu, select **Options**, click
> the **Edit** tab, and click the **When Selecting**, **Automatically
> Select Entire Word** check box to turn it off. Click **OK**.

MOVING TEXT IN THE OUTLINE PANE

As you work in the Normal view, you also can view your presentation
slides as an outline using the Outline pane. This provides you with a
quick way to move text items around on a slide or move them from
slide to slide. Just select the text and drag it to a new position.

As already mentioned, you also can drag text from one slide to another. All you have to do is select a line of text in the Outline pane and drag it to another slide. You also can move a slide in the Outline pane. Drag the slide's icon in the Outline pane to a new position (under the heading for another slide).

If you aren't that confident with your dragging skills, PowerPoint provides help in the form of the Outlining toolbar. It provides buttons that make it easy to move text up or down on a slide (with respect to other text on the slide) or to move a slide up or down in the presentation.

To turn on the Outlining toolbar, right-click one of the PowerPoint toolbars and select **Outlining**. Figure 4.5 shows the Outlining toolbar on the left side of the Outline pane (the Outline pane has also been expanded to take up more of the PowerPoint window).

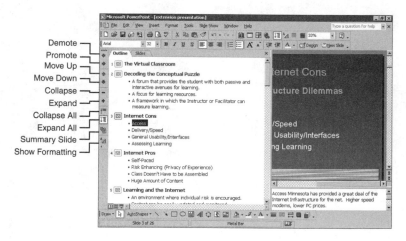

FIGURE 4.5
You can use the Outlining toolbar to move text and slides in the presentation.

- To move a paragraph or text line up in a slide, select it and click the **Move Up** button.

- To move a paragraph or text down in a slide, select it and click the **Move Down** button.

You also can use the **Move Up** and **Move Down** buttons to move entire slides up or down in the presentation. Click the slide's icon, and then use the appropriate button (it might take several clicks to move a slide up or down with respect to another slide).

If you want to see how the text is actually formatted on the slides that you are viewing in the Outline pane, click the **Show Formatting** button on the Outlining toolbar. Viewing the text as it is formatted can help you determine where the text should appear on a slide as you move the text (or whether you will have to reformat the text later).

REARRANGING TEXT IN THE OUTLINE PANE

As you can see from Figure 4.5, your presentation is organized in a multilevel outline format. The slides are at the top level of the outline, and each slide's contents are subordinate under that slide. Some slides have multiple levels of subordination (for example, a bulleted list within a bulleted list).

You can easily change an object's level in Outline view with the Tab key or the Outlining toolbar:

- To demote a paragraph in the outline, click the text, and then press the **Tab** key or click the **Demote** button on the Outlining toolbar.

- To promote a paragraph in the outline, click the text, and then press **Shift+Tab** or click the **Promote** button on the Outlining toolbar.

In most cases, subordinate items on a slide appear as items in a bulleted list. In Lesson 9, "Creating Columns, Tables, and Lists," you learn how to change the appearance of the bullet and the size and formatting of text for each entry, as well as how much the text is indented for each level.

TIP

> **Create Summary Slides in the Outline Pane**   If you would like to create a summary slide for your presentation that contains the headings from several slides, select those slides in the Outline pane (click the first slide, and then hold down the Shift key and click the last slide you want to select). Then, click the **Summary Slide** button on the Outlining toolbar. A new slide appears at the beginning of the selected slides containing the headings from the selected slides. You then can position the Summary slide anywhere in the presentation as you would any other slide.

In this lesson, you learned how to change views for a presentation, move from slide to slide, and edit text. In the next lesson, you learn how to change the look of your slides and the presentation.

Lesson 5

Changing a Presentation's Look

In this lesson, you learn various ways to give your presentation a professional and consistent look.

Giving Your Slides a Professional Look

PowerPoint comes with dozens of professionally created designs and color schemes that you can apply to your presentations. These designs include background patterns, color choices, font choices, and more. When you apply a design template to your presentation, it applies its formatting to a special slide called the Slide Master.

The Slide Master is not really a slide, but it looks like one. It is a master design grid to which you make changes; these changes affect every slide in the presentation. When you apply a template, you actually are applying the template to the Slide Master, which in turn applies it to each slide in the presentation.

PLAIN ENGLISH

Slide Master   A slide that contains the master layout and color scheme for the slides in a presentation.

You don't have to work with the Slide Master itself when you apply template or color scheme changes to your presentations. Just be aware that you can open the Slide Master (select **View**, point at **Master**, and then select **Slide Master**) and change the style and fonts used by the text boxes in a presentation (see Figure 5.1). You also can select a custom background color for the slides in the presentation. Any changes

that you make to the Slide Master affect all the slides in the
presentation.

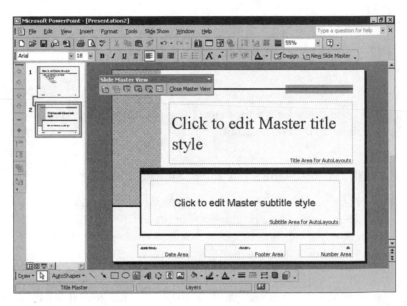

FIGURE 5.1
*The Slide Master holds the default design and color options for the entire
presentation.*

You probably will find that PowerPoint provides enough template and
color scheme options that you won't need to format the Slide Master
itself very often. Edit its properties only if you have a very strict formatting need for the presentation that isn't covered in the templates
and color schemes provided. For example, one good reason to edit the
Slide Master would be a situation in which you want a graphic to
appear on every slide (such as a company logo); you can place the
image on the Slide Master instead of pasting it onto each slide
individually.

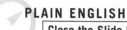

PLAIN ENGLISH

Close the Slide Master   If you open the Slide Master, you can close it by clicking **Close Master View** on the Master View toolbar.

APPLYING A DIFFERENT DESIGN TEMPLATE

You can apply a different template to your presentation at any time, no matter how you originally created the presentation. To change the design template, follow these steps:

1. Select **Format**, **Slide Design** to open the Slide Design task pane. Then, if necessary, click the **Design Templates** icon at the top of the task pane. This provides a listing of PowerPoint's many design templates (see Figure 5.2).

FIGURE 5.2
Choose a different template from the Design Templates task pane.

2. Click the template that you want to use in the list. The template is immediately applied to the slide in the Slide pane.

3. When you have decided on a particular template (you can click on any number of templates to see how they affect your slides), save the presentation (click the **Save** button on the toolbar).

CAUTION

> **The Design Template Changes Custom Formatting**   If you spent time bolding text items on a slide or changing font colors, these changes are affected (lost) when you select a new design template. For example, if you have customized bold items in black in your original design template and switch to another template that uses white text, you lose your customizations. You should choose your design template early in the process of creating your presentation. Then, you can do any customized formatting at the end of the process so that it is not affected by a design template change.

When you work with design templates, you can apply them to all the slides in the presentation (as discussed in the steps provided in this section), or you can apply the template to selected slides in the presentation. Follow these steps to apply a template to a selected group of slides in a presentation:

1. Switch to the Slide Sorter view (select **View**, **Slide Sorter**).

2. Open the Slide Design task pane as outlined in the previous steps.

3. Now you must select the slide (or slides) to which you want to apply the template. Click the first slide you want to select, and then hold down the **Ctrl** key as you click other slides you want to select.

4. Point at the design template you want to use in the Slide Design task pane; a drop-down arrow appears.

5. Click the template's drop-down arrow and select **Apply to Selected Slides** (see Figure 5.3).

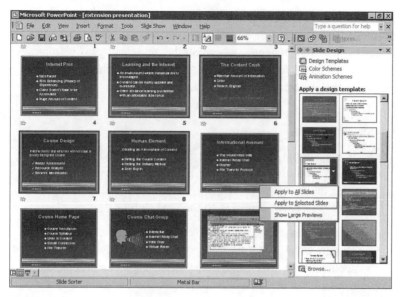

FIGURE 5.3
Design templates can be assigned to selected slides in a presentation.

The template's design then is applied to the selected slides.

TIP

> **View a Larger Design Sample**   To expand the view of the
> design templates, click the drop-down arrow on the tem-
> plate and select **Show Large Previews**.

USING COLOR SCHEMES

Design templates enable you to change the overall design and color
scheme applied to the slides in the presentation (or selected slides in
the presentation, as discussed in the previous section). If you like the
overall design of the slides in the presentation but would like to
explore some other color options, you can select a different color
scheme for the particular template you are using.

The number of color schemes available for a particular design template depends on the template itself. Some templates provide only three or four color schemes, whereas other templates provide more. As with design templates, you can assign a new color scheme to all the slides in the presentation or to selected slides.

To change the color scheme for the presentation or selected slides, follow these steps:

1. In the Normal or Slide Sorter view (use the Slide Sorter view if you want to change the color scheme for selected slides), open the task pane by selecting **View, Task Pane**. (If the task pane is already open, skip to the next step.)

2. Select the task pane's drop-down arrow, and then select **Slide Design-Color Schemes**. This switches to the Color Schemes section of the Slide Design task pane. The color schemes available for the design template that you are using appear in the Apply a Color Scheme section (see Figure 5.4).

3. (Optional) If you are in the Slide Sorter view and want to assign a new color scheme only to selected slides, select those slides (click the first slide and then hold down **Ctrl** and click additional slides).

4. To assign the new color scheme to all the slides in the presentation, click a scheme in the Slide Design task pane. If you are assigning the color scheme only to selected slides, point at the color scheme and click its drop-down arrow. Select **Apply to Selected Slides**.

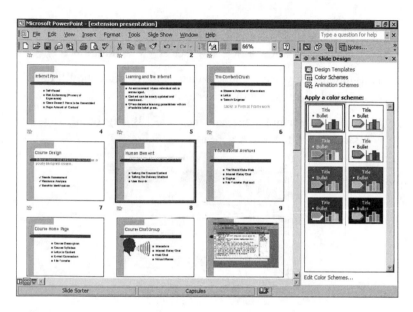

FIGURE 5.4
You can choose from a list of color schemes for the presentation or selected slides.

The new color scheme is applied to the slides in the presentation (or selected slides in the presentation). If you decide you don't like the color scheme, select another scheme from the task pane.

CHANGING THE BACKGROUND FILL

You can fine-tune the color scheme that you add to a slide or slides by changing the background fill. This works best in cases where the design template and color scheme that you selected don't provide a background color for the slide or slides. You must be careful, however, because you don't want to pick a background color that obscures the texts and graphics that you place on the slide or slides.

To change the background fill on a slide or slides, follow these steps:

1. Switch to the Slide Sorter view (select **View**, **Slide Sorter**).

2. (Optional) If you are going to change the background fill for selected slides, select those slides in the Slide Sorter window.

3. Select the **Format** menu, and then select **Background**. The Background dialog box appears (see Figure 5.5).

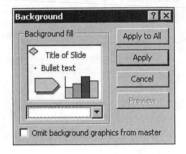

FIGURE 5.5
Use the Background dialog box to add a fill color to a slide or slides.

4. Click the drop-down arrow at the bottom of the dialog box and choose a fill color from the color palette that appears.

5. To assign the fill color to all the slides in the presentation, click **Apply to All**. To assign the fill color to selected slides (if you selected slides in step 2), click **Apply**.

In this lesson, you learned how to give your presentation a consistent look with design templates and color schemes. You also learned how add a fill color to a slide or slides. In the next lesson, you learn how to insert, delete, and copy slides, and you learn to add slides from another presentation.

LESSON 6
Inserting, Deleting, and Copying Slides

In this lesson, you learn how to insert new slides, delete slides, and copy slides in a presentation.

INSERTING A NEW SLIDE

You can insert a slide into a presentation at any time and at any position in the presentation. To insert a new slide, follow these steps:

1. On the Outline or Slides panes, select the slide that appears just before the place you want to insert the new slide (you also can insert a new slide in the Slide Sorter view).

2. Choose the **Insert** menu and then **New Slide**, or click the **New Slide** button on the PowerPoint toolbar. A new blank slide appears in the PowerPoint window, along with the Slide Layout task pane (see Figure 6.1).

3. In the Slide Layout task pane, select the slide layout that you want to use for the new slide. Several text slide layouts and layouts for slides that contain graphics are provided.

New Slide button

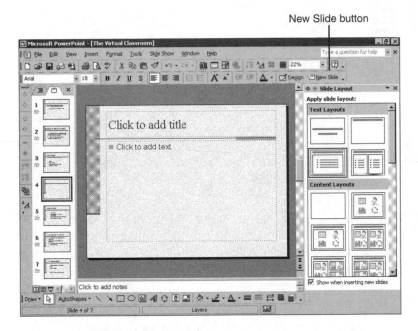

FIGURE 6.1
Your new slide appears in the PowerPoint window.

4. Follow the directions indicated on the slide in the Slide pane to add text or other objects. For text boxes, click an area to select it and then type in your text. For other object placeholders, double-click the placeholder.

PLAIN ENGLISH

Cloning a Slide   To create an exact replica of an existing slide (in any view), select the slide you want to duplicate. Click **Insert**, and then select **Duplicate Slide**. The new slide is inserted after the original slide. You then can choose a different layout for the slide if you want.

INSERTING SLIDES FROM ANOTHER PRESENTATION

If you want to insert some or all of the slides from another presentation into the current presentation, perform these steps:

1. Open the presentation into which you want to insert the slides.

2. Select the slide located before the position where you want to insert the slides.

3. Select the **Insert** menu and select **Slides from Files**. The Slide Finder dialog box appears (see Figure 6.2).

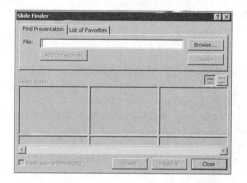

FIGURE 6.2
Use the Slide Finder dialog box to insert slides from another presentation.

4. Click the **Browse** button to display the Browse dialog box. In the Browse dialog box, locate the presentation that contains the slides that you want to insert into the current presentation (use the **Look In** drop-down arrow to switch drives, if necessary).

5. When you locate the presentation, double-click it.

6. The slides in the presentation appear in the Slide Finder's Select Slides box. To select the slides that you want to insert into the current presentation, click the first slide, and then hold down **Ctrl** and click any subsequent slides.

7. When you have selected all the slides you want to insert, click **Insert** (if you want to insert all the slides, click **Insert All**).

8. PowerPoint inserts the slides into the presentation at the point you originally selected. Click **OK** to close the Slide Finder dialog box.

CREATING SLIDES FROM A DOCUMENT OUTLINE

If you have created a document in Word that includes outline-style headings and numbered or bulleted lists, PowerPoint can pull the headings and the text from the document and create slides. To create slides from a document outline, follow these steps:

1. Choose the **Insert** menu, and then choose **Slides from Outline**. The Insert Outline dialog box appears (it is similar to the Open dialog box used to open a presentation or other file).

2. Use the Insert Outline dialog box to locate the document file you want to use.

3. Double-click the name of the document file.

PowerPoint then uses all the first-level headings to create slides for your presentation. Any text in the document below a first-level outline heading is added to the slide in an additional text box.

SELECTING SLIDES

In the following sections, you learn how to delete, copy, and move slides. However, before you can do anything with a slide, you must select it. To select slides, follow these directions:

- To select a single slide, click it.

- To select two or more contiguous slides in the Outline pane, click the first slide, and then hold down the **Shift** key while you click the last slide in the group.

- To select two or more contiguous slides in the Slides pane or the Slide Sorter view, place the mouse pointer in front of the first slide you want to select (not on it), and drag to select additional slides.

CAUTION

> **Don't Drag the Slide**   If you are trying to select multiple, contiguous slides by dragging with the mouse, drag from in front of the first slide. Don't start dragging while pointing directly at the first slide because it will move the slide rather than highlight the remaining slides that you want to select.

- To select multiple noncontiguous slides in Slide Sorter view, click the first slide and hold down the **Ctrl** key while clicking subsequent slides in the group.

DELETING SLIDES

You can delete a slide from any view. To delete a slide, perform the following steps:

1. Select the slide you want to delete. You can delete multiple slides by selecting more than one slide (on the Outline or Slides pane or in the Slide Sorter view).

2. Choose the **Edit** menu, and then choose **Delete Slide**. The slide is removed from the presentation.

TIP

> **Use the Delete Key**   You can quickly delete slides by selecting the slide or slides and then pressing the **Delete** key on the keyboard.

CAUTION

> **Oops!** If you deleted a slide by mistake, you can get it back. Select **Edit**, **Undo**, or press **Ctrl+Z**. This works only if you do it immediately. You cannot undo the change if you exit PowerPoint and restart the application.

CUTTING, COPYING, AND PASTING SLIDES

In Lesson 7, "Rearranging Slides in a Presentation," you learn how to rearrange slides using the Slide Sorter and the Outline/Slides pane. Although dragging slides to new positions in the Slide Sorter is probably the easiest way to move slides, you can use the Cut, Copy, and Paste commands to move or copy slides in the presentation. Follow these steps:

1. Change to Slide Sorter view, or display Normal view and work with the Outline or Slides panes.

2. Select the slides you want to copy or cut.

3. Open the **Edit** menu and select **Cut** or **Copy** to either move or copy the slides, respectively, or you can use the **Cut** or **Copy** toolbar buttons.

TIP

> **Quick Cut or Copy** From the keyboard, press **Ctrl+C** to copy or **Ctrl+X** to cut.

4. In Slide Sorter view, select the slide after which you want to place the cut or copied slides, or on the Outline pane, move the insertion point to the end of the text in the slide after which you want to insert the cut or copied slides.

5. Choose the **Edit** menu and choose **Paste**, or click the **Paste** toolbar button. PowerPoint inserts the cut or copied slides.

TIP

Keyboard Shortcut   You also can press **Ctrl+V** to paste an item that you cut or copied.

In this lesson, you learned how to insert, delete, cut, copy, and paste slides. In the next lesson, you learn how to rearrange the slides in your presentation.

LESSON 7

Rearranging Slides in a Presentation

In this lesson, you learn how to rearrange your slides using the Slide Sorter view and the Outline/Slides pane.

REARRANGING SLIDES IN SLIDE SORTER VIEW

Slide Sorter view shows thumbnails of the slides in your presentation. This enables you to view many if not all slides in the presentation at one time. Slide Sorter view provides the ideal environment for arranging slides in the appropriate order for your presentation. To rearrange slides in Slide Sorter view, perform the following steps:

1. If necessary, switch to Slide Sorter view by selecting **View** and then choosing **Slide Sorter**.

2. Place the mouse pointer on the slide you want to move.

3. Hold down the left mouse button and drag the slide to a new position in the presentation. The mouse pointer becomes a small slide box.

4. To position the slide, place the mouse before or after another slide in the presentation. A vertical line appears before or after the slide (see Figure 7.1).

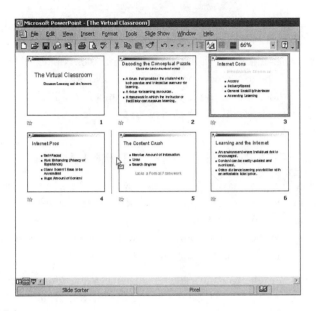

FIGURE 7.1
Drag a slide in the presentation to a new position.

CAUTION

Destination Not in View? If you have more than just a few slides in your presentation, you might not be able to see the slide's final destination in the Slide Sorter. Don't worry; just drag the slide in the direction of the destination, and the Slide Sorter pane scrolls in that direction.

5. Release the mouse button. PowerPoint places the slide into its new position and shifts the surrounding slides to make room for the inserted slide.

You can copy a slide in Slide Sorter view as easily as you can move a slide. Simply hold down the **Ctrl** key while you drag the slide. When you release the mouse, PowerPoint inserts a copy of the selected slide into the presentation.

Although the Slides pane on the left side of the Normal view window does not provide as much workspace as the Slide Sorter, you can use the techniques discussed in this section to move or copy a slide. The Slides pane probably works best when you have only a few slides in the presentation. When you have a large number of slides, you might want to switch from the Normal view to the Slide Sorter view.

REARRANGING SLIDES IN THE OUTLINE PANE

In the Outline pane of the Normal view, you see the presentation as an outline that numbers each slide and shows its title and slide text. This provides you with a pretty good picture of the content and overall organization of your presentation. To rearrange the slides in your presentation using the Outline pane, follow these steps:

1. Switch to the Normal view by selecting **View**, **Normal**, or by clicking the **Normal** button on the bottom left of the PowerPoint window.

2. Click the slide number you want to move. This highlights the contents of the entire slide.

3. Place the mouse on the slide icon for that particular slide and drag the slide up or down within the presentation; then release the mouse.

 TIP

> **Use the Up or Down Buttons**   You also can move a slide in the outline by selecting the slide and then using the **Move Up** or **Move Down** buttons on the Outlining toolbar.

HIDING SLIDES

Before you give a presentation, you should try to anticipate any questions that your audience might have and be prepared to answer those questions. You might even want to create slides to support your

answers to these questions and then keep the slides hidden until you
need them. To hide one or more slides, perform the following steps:

1. In the Slide Sorter view or the Slides pane of the Normal
   view, select the slides you want to hide.

2. Select the **Slide Show** menu, and then select **Hide Slide**. In
   the Slide Sorter view and in the Slides pane, the hidden
   slide's number appears in a box with a line through it (see
   Figure 7.2).

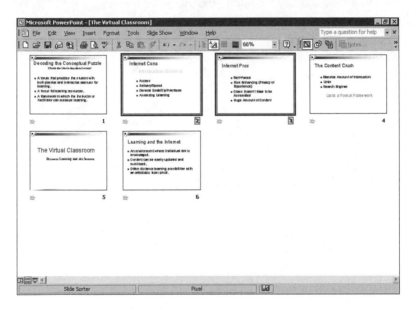

FIGURE 7.2
*Hidden slides are denoted by a line through the slide number (slides 2 and 3 in
this figure).*

3. To unhide the slides, display or select the hidden slides,
   choose the **Slide Show** menu, and then select **Hide Slide**.

TIP

Right-Click Shortcut   To quickly hide a slide, you can right-click it and select **Hide Slide** from the shortcut menu that appears. To unhide the slide, right-click it again and select **Hide Slide** again.

In this lesson, you learned how to rearrange the slides in a presentation and how to hide slides. In the next lesson, you learn how to add text to a slide and how to modify the text in text boxes.

LESSON 8
Adding and Modifying Slide Text

In this lesson, you learn how to add text boxes to a slide and change the text alignment and line spacing.

CREATING A TEXT BOX

As you learned in Lesson 4, "Working with Slides in Different Views," the text on slides resides in various text boxes. To edit the text in a text box, click in the box to place the insertion point, and then enter or edit the text within the box. If you want to add additional text to a slide that will not be contained in one of the text boxes already on the slide, you must create a new text box.

PLAIN ENGLISH

> **Text Box** A text box acts as a receptacle for the text. Text boxes often contain bulleted lists, notes, and labels (used to point to important parts of illustrations).

To create a text box, perform the following steps:

1. If necessary, switch to the Normal view (select **View**, **Normal**). Use the Slides or Outline tab on the left of the workspace to select the slide on which you want to work. The slide appears in the Slide pane.

2. Click the **Text Box** button on the Drawing toolbar (if the Drawing toolbar isn't visible, right-click any toolbar and select **Drawing**).

3. Click the slide where you want the text box to appear. A small text box appears (see Figure 8.1). (It will expand as you type in it.)

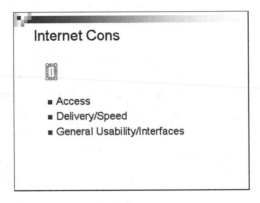

FIGURE 8.1
Text boxes can be inserted from the Drawing toolbar.

4. Type the text that you want to appear in the text box. Press **Enter** to start a new paragraph. Don't worry if the text box becomes too wide; you can resize it when you are finished typing.

5. When you are finished, click anywhere outside the text box to see how the text appears on the finished slide.

6. If you want, drag the text box's selection handles to resize it. If you make the box narrower, text within a paragraph might wrap to the next line.

If the text does not align correctly in the text box, see the section "Changing the Text Alignment and Line Spacing," later in this lesson, to learn how to change it.

TIP

> **Rotate a Text Box**   You can rotate a text box using the green rotation handle that appears at the top center of a selected text box. Place the mouse pointer on the handle, and the rotation icon appears. Use the mouse to drag the rotation handle to the desired position to rotate the box.

CHANGING FONT ATTRIBUTES

You can enhance your text by using the Font dialog box or by using various tools on the Formatting toolbar. Use the Font dialog box if you want to add several enhancements to your text at one time. Use the Formatting toolbar to add one font enhancement at a time.

PLAIN ENGLISH

> **Fonts, Styles, and Effects**   In PowerPoint, a font is a family of text that has the same design or typeface (for example, Arial or Courier). A style is a standard enhancement, such as bold or italic. An effect is a special enhancement, such as shadow or underline.

USING THE FONT DIALOG BOX

The font dialog box offers you control over all the attributes you can apply to text. Attributes such as strikethrough, superscript, subscript, and shadow are available as check boxes in this dialog box.

You can change the font of existing text or of text you are about to type by performing the following steps:

1. To change the font of existing text, select text by clicking and dragging the I-beam pointer over the text in a particular text box. If you want to change font attributes for all the text in a text box, select the text box (do not place the insertion point within the text box).

2. Choose the **Format** menu, and then choose **Font**. The Font dialog box appears, as shown in Figure 8.2.

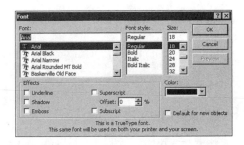

FIGURE 8.2
The Font dialog box enables you to change all the text attributes for selected text.

TIP

> **Right-Click Quick**   You can right-click the text and select **Font** from the shortcut menu to open the Font dialog box.

3. From the Font list, select the font you want to use.

4. From the Font Style list, select any style you want to apply to the text, such as Bold or Italic. (To remove styles from text, select **Regular**.)

5. From the Size list, select any size in the list, or type a size directly into the box. (With TrueType fonts—the fonts marked with the TT logo—you can type any point size, even sizes that do not appear on the list.)

6. In the Effects box, select any special effects you want to add to the text, such as **Underline**, **Shadow**, or **Emboss**. You also can choose **Superscript** or **Subscript**, although these are less common.

7. To change the color of your text, click the arrow button to the right of the Color list and click the desired color. (For more

colors, click the **More Colors** option at the bottom of the
Color drop-down list; to select a color, use the dialog box
that appears.)

8. Click **OK** to apply the new look to your selected text.

TIP

> **Title and Object Area Text**   If you change a font on an
> individual slide, the font change applies only to that
> slide. To change the font for all the slides in the presen-
> tation, you must change the font on the Slide Master.
> Select **View**, point at **Master**, and then select **Slide
> Master**. Select a text area and perform the preceding
> steps to change the look of the text on all slides. Be
> careful, however, because these changes override any
> font styles that are supplied by the design template
> assigned to the presentation.

FORMATTING TEXT WITH THE FORMATTING TOOLBAR

The Formatting toolbar provides several buttons that enable you to
change font attributes for the text on your slides. It makes it easy for
you to quickly bold selected text or to change the color of text in a
text box.

To use the different Formatting toolbar font tools, follow these steps:

1. To change the look of existing text, select the text, or select a
    particular text box to change the look of all the text within
    that box.

2. To change fonts, open the **Font** drop-down list and click the
    desired font.

3. To change font size, open the **Font Size** drop-down list, click
    the desired size or type a size directly into the box, and then
    press **Enter**.

Incrementing the Type Size   To increase or decrease the text size to the next size up or down, click the **Increase Font Size** or **Decrease Font Size** buttons on the Formatting toolbar.

4. To add a style or effect to the text (bold, italic, underline, and/or shadow), click the appropriate button(s):

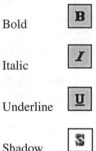

Bold

Italic

Underline

Shadow

As you have already seen, you can change the font color through the Font dialog box. You also can change it with the **Font Color** button on the Formatting toolbar. Just do the following:

1. Select the text for which you want to change the color.

2. Click the down-pointing arrow next to the **Font Color** button on the Formatting toolbar. A color palette appears (see Figure 8.3).

3. Do one of the following:

- Click a color on the palette to change the color of the selected text or the text box (the colors available are based on the design template and color scheme you have selected for the presentation).

- Click the **More Font Colors** option to display a Colors dialog box. Click a color on the Standard tab or use the Custom tab to create your own color. Then click **OK**. The color is applied to the text.

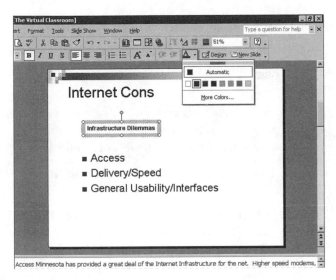

FIGURE 8.3
When you click the arrow next to the Font Colors button, a color palette appears.

COPYING TEXT FORMATS

If your presentation contains text with a format you want to use, you can copy that text's format and apply it to other text on the slide (or other slides). To copy text formats, perform the following steps:

1. Highlight the text with the format you want to use.

2. Click the **Format Painter** button on the toolbar. PowerPoint copies the format.

3. Drag the mouse pointer (which now looks like the Format Painter icon) across the text to which you want to apply the format.

If you want to apply a format to different text lines or even different text boxes on a slide or slides, double-click the **Format Painter** button. Use the mouse to apply styles to as many text items as you want. Then, click the **Format Painter** button again to turn off the feature.

CHANGING THE TEXT ALIGNMENT AND LINE SPACING

When you first type text, PowerPoint automatically places it against the left edge of the text box. To change the paragraph alignment, perform the following steps:

1. Click anywhere inside the paragraph you want to realign (a paragraph is any text line or wrapped text lines followed by a line break—created when you press the **Enter** key).

2. Select the **Format** menu, and then select **Alignment**. The Alignment submenu appears (see Figure 8.4).

3. Select **Align Left**, **Center**, **Align Right**, or **Justify** to align the paragraph as required.

FIGURE 8.4
You can align each text line or paragraph in a text box.

TIP

> **Some Alignment Shortcuts** To quickly set left alignment, press **Ctrl+L** or click the **Align Left** button on the Formatting toolbar. For centered alignment, press **Ctrl+C** or click the **Center** button. For right alignment, press **Ctrl+R** or click the **Align Right** button.

If you want to align all the text in a text box in the same way (rather than aligning the text line by line), select the entire text box (click the box border), and then use the Alignment menu selection or the alignment buttons on the Formatting toolbar.

You also can change the spacing between text lines (remember, PowerPoint considers these to be paragraphs) in a text box. The default setting for line spacing is single space. To change the line spacing in a paragraph, perform these steps:

1. Click inside the paragraph you want to change, or select all the paragraphs you want to change by selecting the entire text box.

2. Select **Format, Line Spacing**. The Line Spacing dialog box appears, as shown in Figure 8.5.

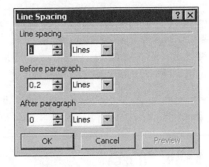

FIGURE 8.5
Select Format, Line Spacing to open the Line Spacing dialog box.

3. Click the arrow buttons to the right of any of the following text boxes to change the spacing for the following:

   • **Line Spacing**—This setting controls the space between the lines in a paragraph.

   • **Before Paragraph**—This setting controls the space between this paragraph and the paragraph that comes before it.

   • **After Paragraph**—This setting controls the space between this paragraph and the paragraph that comes after it.

4. After you make your selections, click **OK**.

PLAIN ENGLISH

> **Lines or Points?**   The drop-down list box that appears to the right of each setting enables you to set the line spacing in lines or points. A line is the current line height (based on the current text size). A point is a unit commonly used to measure text. One point is 1/72 of an inch.

SELECTING, DELETING, AND MOVING A TEXT BOX

If you go back and click anywhere inside the text box, a selection box appears around it. If you click the selection box border, handles appear around the text box. You can drag the box's border to move the box or drag a handle to resize it. PowerPoint wraps the text automatically as needed to fit inside the box.

To delete a text box, select it (so that handles appear around it and no insertion point appears inside it), and then press the **Delete** key.

ADDING A WORDART OBJECT

PowerPoint comes with an add-on program called WordArt (which also is available in other Office applications, such as Word and Excel) that can help you create graphical text effects. You can create text wrapped in a circle and text that has 3D effects and other special alignment options. To insert a WordArt object onto a slide, perform the following steps:

1. In the Slide view, display the slide on which you want to place the WordArt object.

2. Click the **Insert** menu, point at **Picture**, and then select **WordArt**. The WordArt Gallery dialog box appears, showing many samples of WordArt types.

3. Click the sample that best represents the WordArt type you want, and click **OK**. The Edit WordArt Text dialog box appears (see Figure 8.6).

FIGURE 8.6
Enter the text, size, and font to be used into the Edit WordArt Text dialog box.

4. Choose a font and size from the respective drop-down lists.

5. Type the text you want to use into the Text box.

6. Click **OK**. PowerPoint creates the WordArt text on your slide, as shown in Figure 8.7.

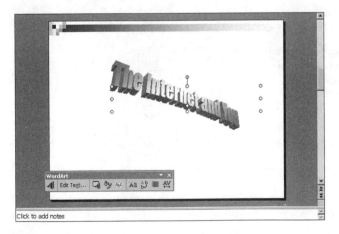

FIGURE 8.7
The WordArt toolbar is available when your WordArt object is selected.

After you have created WordArt, you have access to the WordArt toolbar, shown in Figure 8.7. You can use it to modify your WordArt. Table 8.1 summarizes the toolbar's buttons.

Table 8.1   Buttons on the WordArt Toolbar

To Do This	Click This
Insert a new WordArt object	
Edit the text, size, and font of the selected WordArt object	Edit Text...
Change the style of the current WordArt object in the WordArt Gallery	
Open a Format WordArt dialog box	
Change the shape of the WordArt	Abc
Make all the letters the same height	Aa
Toggle between vertical and horizontal text orientation	Ab bↄ
Change the text alignment	
Change the spacing between letters	AV

You can rotate a WordArt object by dragging the rotation handle on the WordArt box. To edit the WordArt object, double-click it to display the WordArt toolbar and text entry box. Enter your changes, and then click outside the WordArt object. You can move the object by dragging its border or resize it by dragging a handle.

In this lesson, you learned how to add text to a slide, how to change the text alignment and spacing, and how to add WordArt objects. You also learned how to change the appearance of text by changing its font, size, style, and color. In addition, you learned how to copy text formats. In the next lesson, you learn how to use tables and tabs to create columns and lists.

LESSONS 9
Creating Columns, Tables, and Lists

In this lesson, you learn how to use tabs to create columns of text, bulleted lists, numbered lists, and other types of lists.

WORKING IN MULTIPLE COLUMNS

Depending on the type of slide you are creating, you might find the occasion to arrange text on a slide in multiple columns. PowerPoint provides three options for placing text into columns on a slide:

- You can use the Title and 2 Column slide layout to create a slide with side-by-side text columns.

- You can place tab stops in a single text box and press Tab to create columns for your text.

- You can use a table to create a two- or multiple-column text grid.

In this lesson, you learn about all these methods.

CREATING COLUMNS WITH A SLIDE LAYOUT

The easiest way to create columns of text is to change a slide's layout so that it provides side-by-side text boxes. Because the default layout for slides is a slide with a title box and a single text box, you probably will need to use the Slide Layout task pane to change its format to include two text columns. Follow these steps:

1. Create a new slide or select a slide that you want to format with the two-column layout (using the Outline or Slides pane).

2. Open the task pane (select **View**, **Task Pane**).

3. Select the task pane drop-down arrow and select **Slide Layout**.

4. Click the **Title and 2 Column** slide layout from the Text Layouts section of the Slide Layout task pane to format the slide (see Figure 9.1).

FIGURE 9.1
A two-column slide layout provides two panes in which to enter text.

You then can type the text that you want to appear in the two text boxes provided on the slide.

Place the Mouse on a Slide Layout to See Its Description
If you place the mouse on any of the slide layouts in the
Slide Layout task pane, a tip appears, describing the
layout.

USING TABS TO CREATE COLUMNS

You can create multiple columns in a text box using tab stops. To set
the tabs for a multicolumn list, perform the following steps:

1. Open the presentation and select the slide with which you
   want to work in Slide view.

 2. Create a text box for the text if one does not already exist
   (use the **Text Box** icon on the Drawing toolbar to create the
   text box).

Disappearing Text Box   If you are creating a brand-new
text box in step 2, type a few characters in it to anchor
it to the slide. Otherwise, it disappears when you click
outside it, meaning it no longer exists and you will have
to insert it all over again.

3. Click anywhere inside the text box. After the insertion point
   is in the text box, you can set the tabs.

4. If you already typed text inside the text box, select the text.

5. If the ruler is not onscreen, select the **View** menu, and then
   select **Ruler** to display the ruler.

6. Click the **Tab** button at the left end of the ruler until it represents the type of tab you want to set (see Table 9.1 for more
   information on the type of tabs available).

7. Click in various positions on the ruler to place a tab stop using the type of tab you currently have selected. Figure 9.2 shows several tab stops that have been placed in a text box.

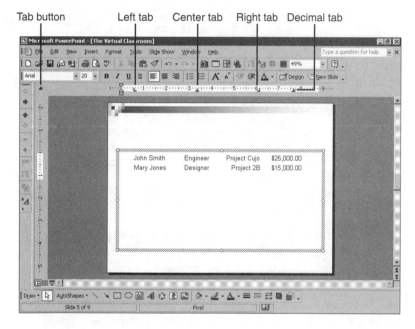

FIGURE 9.2
The ruler enables you to create tab stops for a text box.

8. Repeat steps 6 and 7 if you want to set different types of tab stops at different positions.

9. To change the position of an existing tab stop setting, drag it on the ruler to the desired position. To delete an existing tab stop setting, drag it off the ruler.

10. (Optional) To hide the ruler, select the **View** menu and then select **Ruler**.

Table 9.1   Tab Button Stop Types

Button Appearance	Tab Stop Type
L	Aligns the left end of the line against the tab stop.
⊥	Centers the text on the tab stop.
⅃	Aligns the right end of the line against the tab stop.
⊥	Aligns the tab stop on a period. This is called a decimal tab and is useful for aligning a column of numbers that uses decimal points.

CREATING A TABLE

Tables can also be used to place text in side-by-side columns. You can create tables that provide two columns, three columns, or any number of columns that you require. Tables are also very useful when you want to display numerical information in a grid layout or information that you want to arrange in rows. A table is a collection of intersecting columns and rows. The block created when a column and a row intersects often is referred to as a *cell*. The easiest way to create a table on a slide is to use the Table layout. Follow these steps:

1. Create a new slide or select a slide that you want to format with the Table layout (using the Outline or Slides pane).

2. Open the task pane (select **View**, **Task Pane**).

3. Select the task pane drop-down arrow and select **Slide Layout**.

4. Scroll down through the slide layouts in the task pane, and then click the **Title and Table** layout. This assigns the Title and Table layout to the current slide (see Figure 9.3).

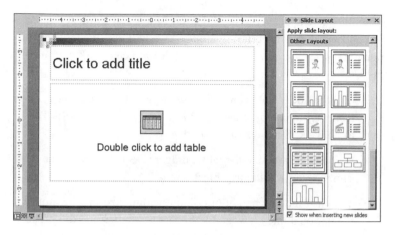

FIGURE 9.3
The Table layout enables you to place a table on a slide.

5. After you assign the Title and Table layout to the slide, you can set the number of columns and rows for the table. Double-click the Table icon on the slide. The Insert dialog box appears.

6. Specify the number of columns and rows that you want in the table, and then click **OK**. The table is placed on the slide.

You also can insert a table onto an existing slide. This enables you to include a table on a slide where you don't want to change the slide's layout as discussed in the preceding steps. Follow these steps:

1. Display the slide on which you want to place the table.

2. Select the **Insert** menu and choose **Table**. The Insert Table dialog box appears.

3. Enter the number of columns and rows that you want to have in the table.

4. Click **OK**. The table appears on the slide.

When the table appears on the slide, the Tables and Borders toolbar also appears in the PowerPoint window (we will use this toolbar in a moment). After you have a table on a slide, you can work with it like this:

- Click inside a table cell and enter your text. You can move from cell to cell by pressing **Tab** to go forward or **Shift+Tab** to go back. Enter text as needed.

- If you need to resize the table, drag a selection handle, the same as you would any object.

- To adjust the row height or column width, position the mouse pointer on a line between two rows or columns and drag. The mouse pointer becomes a sizing tool when you place it on any column or row border.

- If you want to change the style of the borders around certain cells on the table (or the entire table), select the cells (drag the mouse across the cells to select them). You then can use the buttons on the Tables and Borders toolbar to change the border attributes (see Figure 9.4). Use the Border Style button and the Border Width button to change the border style and border line weight, respectively. If you want to change the border color, use the Border Color button. The buttons on the Tables and Borders toolbar adjust the thickness and style of the table gridlines.

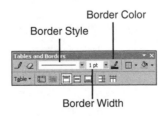

FIGURE 9.4
Border attributes for the table can be changed using the buttons on the Tables and Borders toolbar.

To make a table appear to be multiple columns of text without the table borders, turn off all the gridlines in the table. To do so, select all the cells in the table; then, right-click and choose **Borders and Fill**. In the Format Table dialog box that appears (see Figure 9.5), click each of the border buttons provided on the table diagram to turn the border off for each side of each cell in the table. Click **OK** to return to the table.

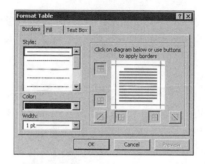

FIGURE 9.5
The Format Table dialog box can be used to control border lines and other table attributes.

MAKING A BULLETED LIST

When you enter new slides into a presentation, the default layout provides a title box and a text box that is set up as a simple bulleted list. Therefore, just creating a new slide creates a bulleted list.

You can turn off the bullets in front of any paragraphs by selecting the paragraphs and clicking the **Bullets** button on the Formatting toolbar to toggle the bullets off. If you want to remove the bullets from all the paragraphs (remember, a text line followed by the Enter key is a paragraph), select the entire text box and click the **Bullets** button.

When you insert your own text boxes using the Text Box button on the Drawing toolbar, the text does not have bullets by default. You can add your own bullets by following these steps:

1. Click the text line (paragraph) that you want to format for bullets. If you want to add bullets to all the text lines in a text box, select the text box.

2. Select the **Format** menu, and then select **Bullets and Numbering**. The Bullets and Numbering dialog box appears (see Figure 9.6).

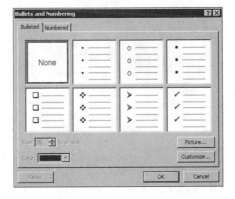

FIGURE 9.6
The Bullets and Numbering dialog box enables you to select the bullets for your bulleted items.

TIP

> **Quick Bullets**   To bypass the dialog box, click the **Bullets** button on the Formatting toolbar to insert a bullet, or right-click and select **Bullet** from the shortcut menu. You can click the **Bullets** button again to remove the bullet.

3. Select the bullet style you want to use from the list Power-Point provides.

4. Click **OK**. PowerPoint formats the selected text into a bulleted list. (If you press **Enter** at the end of a bulleted paragraph, the next paragraph starts with a bullet.)

TIP

> **Create Your Own Bullets**   You can select from a number of pictures and symbols for the bullets that you apply to text in PowerPoint. In the Bullets and Numbering dialog box, select **Picture** to choose from several bullet pictures. Select **Customize** to select from several bullet symbols.

WORKING WITH NUMBERED LISTS

Numbered lists are like bulleted lists, except they have sequential numbers instead of symbols. You can convert any paragraphs to a numbered list by selecting them and clicking the **Numbering** button on the Formatting toolbar. Select the paragraphs again and click the **Numbering** button again to toggle the numbering off.

You also can create numbered lists with the Bullets and Numbering dialog box, the same as you did with bullets. Follow these steps:

1. Select the paragraphs that you want to convert to a numbered list.

2. Choose **Format**, and then select **Bullets and Numbering**.

3. Click the **Numbered** tab on the dialog box. The numbered list styles appear (see Figure 9.7).

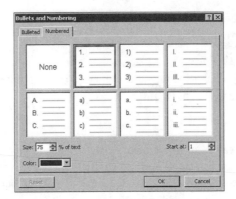

FIGURE 9.7
*Choose the numbering style you want or turn numbering off by choosing **None**.*

4. Click the number style you want for your list.

5. (Optional) Change the Size and/or Color of the numbers.

6. (Optional) If you want the list to start at a number other than 1, enter it into the **Start At** text box.

7. Click **OK**.

In this lesson, you learned how to create columns with slide layouts, tabs, and tables, and how to work with bulleted and numbered lists. In the next lesson, you learn how to get help in PowerPoint.

LESSON 10

Getting Help in Microsoft PowerPoint

In this lesson, you learn how to access and use the Help system in Microsoft PowerPoint.

HELP: WHAT'S AVAILABLE?

Microsoft PowerPoint supplies a Help system that makes it easy for you to look up information on PowerPoint commands and features as you work on your presentations. Because every person is different, the Help system can be accessed in several ways. You can

- Ask a question in the Ask a Question box.

- Ask the Office Assistant for help.

- Get help on a particular element you see onscreen with the What's This? tool.

- Use the Contents, Answer Wizard, and Index tabs in the Help window to get help.

- Access the Office on the Web feature to view Web pages containing help information (if you are connected to the Internet

USING THE ASK A QUESTION BOX

The Ask a Question box is a new way to access the PowerPoint Help system. It also is the easiest way to quickly get help. An Ask a Question box resides at the top right of the PowerPoint window.

For example, if you are working in PowerPoint and want to view information on how to create a chart, type **How do I create a chart?** into the Ask a Question box. Then, press the **Enter** key. A shortcut menu appears below the Ask a Question box, as shown in Figure 10.1.

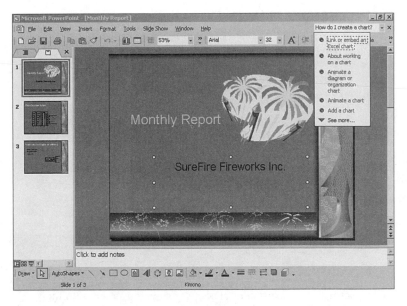

FIGURE 10.1
The Ask a Question box provides a list of Help topics that you can quickly access.

To access one of the Help topics supplied on the shortcut menu, click that particular topic. The Help window opens with topical matches for that keyword or phrase displayed.

In the case of the chart question used in Figure 10.1, you could select **Add a chart** from the shortcut menu that appears. This opens the help window and displays help on how to add a chart to a slide (see Figure 10.2).

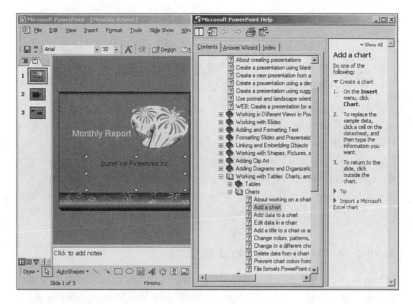

FIGURE 10.2
The Ask a Question box provides a quick way to access the Help window.

In the Help window, you can use the links provided to navigate the Help system. You also can use the Contents, Answer Wizard, and Index tabs to find additional information or look for new information in the Help window. You learn more about these different Help window tabs later in this lesson.

USING THE OFFICE ASSISTANT

Another way to get help in PowerPoint is to use the Office Assistant. The Office Assistant supplies the same type of access to the Help system as the Ask a Question box. You ask the Office Assistant a question, and it supplies you with a list of possible answers that provide links to various Help topics. The next two sections discuss how to use the Office Assistant.

TURNING THE OFFICE ASSISTANT ON AND OFF

By default, the Office Assistant is off. To show the Office Assistant in your application window, select the **Help** menu, and then select **Show the Office Assistant**.

You also can quickly hide the Office Assistant if you no longer want it in your application window. Right-click the Office Assistant and select **Hide**. If you want to get rid of the Office Assistant completely so it isn't activated when you select the Help feature, right-click the Office Assistant and select **Options**. Clear the **Use the Office Assistant** check box, and then click **OK**. You can always get the Office Assistant back by selecting **Help**, **Show Office Assistant**.

ASKING THE OFFICE ASSISTANT A QUESTION

When you click the Office Assistant, a balloon appears above it. Type a question into the text box. For example, you might type `How do I print?` for help printing your work. Click the **Search** button.

The Office Assistant provides some topics that reference Help topics in the Help system. Click the option that best describes what you're trying to do. The Help window appears, containing more detailed information. Use the Help window to get the exact information you need.

Although not everyone likes the Office Assistant because having it enabled means it is always sitting in your PowerPoint window, it can be useful at times. For example, when you access particular features in PowerPoint, the Office Assistant can automatically provide you with context-sensitive help on that particular feature. If you are brand new to Microsoft PowerPoint, you might want to use the Office Assistant to help you learn the various features that PowerPoint provides.

TIP

> **Select Your Own Office Assistant**   Several different Office
> Assistants are available in Microsoft Office. To select
> your favorite, click the Office Assistant and select the
> **Options** button. On the Office Assistant dialog box that
> appears, select the **Gallery** tab. Click the **Next** button
> repeatedly to see the different Office Assistants that are
> available. When you locate the assistant you want to
> use, click **OK**.

USING THE HELP WINDOW

You can forgo either the Type a Question box or the Office Assistant
and get your help directly from the Help window. To directly access
the Help window, select **Help** and then **Microsoft PowerPoint Help**.
You also can press the **F1** key to make the Help window appear.

The Help window provides two panes. The pane on the left provides
three tabs: Contents, Answer Wizard, and Index. The right pane of the
Help window provides either help subject matter or links to different
Help topics. It functions a great deal like a Web browser window. You
click a link to a particular body of information and that information
appears in the right pane.

The first thing you should do is maximize the Help window by clicking its **Maximize** button. This makes it easier to locate and read the
information that the Help system provides (see Figure 10.3).

When you first open the Help window, a group of links in the right
pane provides you with access to information about new PowerPoint
features and other links, such as a link to Microsoft's Office Web site.
Next, take a look at how you can take advantage of different ways to
find information in the Help window: the Contents tab, the Answer
Wizard tab, and the Index tab.

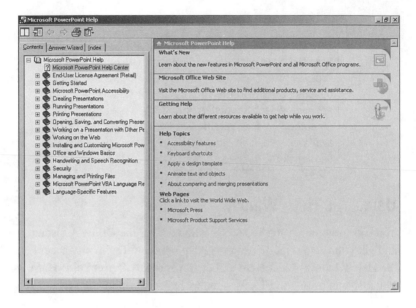

FIGURE 10.3
The Help window provides access to all the help information provided for PowerPoint.

TIP

> **View the Help Window Tabs**   If you don't see the different tabs in the Help window, click the **Show** button on the Help window toolbar.

USING THE CONTENTS TAB

The Contents tab of the Help system is a series of books you can open. Each book has one or more Help topics in it, which appear as pages or chapters. To select a Help topic from the Contents tab, follow these steps:

1. In the Help window, click the **Contents** tab on the left side of the Help window.

2. Find the book that describes, in broad terms, the subject for which you need help.

3. Double-click the book, and a list of Help topics appears below the book, as shown in Figure 10.4.

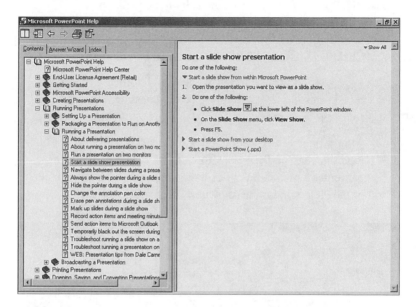

FIGURE 10.4
Use the Contents tab to browse through the various Help topics.

4. Click one of the pages (the pages contain a question mark) under a Help topic to display it in the right pane of the Help window.

5. When you finish reading a topic, select another topic on the Contents tab or click the Help window's **Close** (**x**) button to exit Help.

USING THE ANSWER WIZARD

Another way to get help in the Help window is to use the Answer Wizard. The Answer Wizard works the same as the Ask a Question box or the Office Assistant; you ask the wizard questions and it supplies you with a list of topics that relate to your question. You click one of the choices provided to view help in the Help window.

To get help using the Answer Wizard, follow these steps:

1. Click the **Answer Wizard** tab in the Help window.

2. Type your question into the What Would You Like to Do? box. For example, you might type the question, `How do I insert a new slide?`

3. After typing your question, click the **Search** button. A list of topics appears in the Select Topic to Display box. Select a particular topic, and its information appears in the right pane of the Help window, as shown in Figure 10.5.

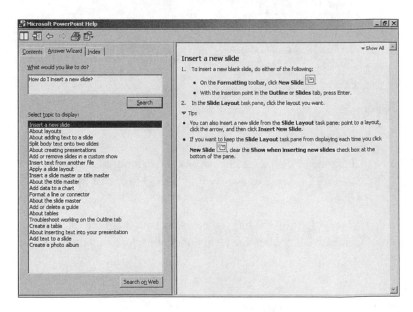

FIGURE 10.5
Search for help in the Help window using the Answer Wizard tab.

TIP

> **Print Help**   If you want to print information provided in the Help window, click the **Print** icon on the Help toolbar.

USING THE INDEX

The index is an alphabetical listing of every Help topic available. It's like an index in a book.

Follow these steps to use the index:

1. In the Help window, click the **Index** tab.

2. Type the first few letters of the topic for which you are looking. The Or Choose Keywords box jumps quickly to a keyword that contains the characters you have typed.

3. Double-click the appropriate keyword in the keywords box. Topics for that keyword appear in the Choose a Topic box.

4. Click a topic to view help in the right pane of the Help window.

TIP

> **Navigation Help Topics**   You can move from topic to topic in the right pane of the Help window by clicking the various links that are provided there. Some topics are collapsed. Click the triangle next to the topic to expand the topic and view the help provided.

GETTING HELP WITH SCREEN ELEMENTS

If you wonder about the function of a particular button or tool on the PowerPoint screen, wonder no more. Just follow these steps to learn about this part of Help:

1. Select **Help** and then **What's This?** or press **Shift+F1**. The mouse pointer changes to an arrow with a question mark.

2. Click the screen element for which you want help. A box
   appears explaining the element.

TIP

> **Take Advantage of ScreenTips**   Another Help feature pro-
> vided by the Office applications is the ScreenTip. All the
> buttons on the different toolbars provided by PowerPoint
> have a ScreenTip. Place the mouse on a particular but-
> ton or icon, and the name of the item (which often helps
> you determine its function) appears in a ScreenTip.

In this lesson you learned how to access the PowerPoint Help feature.
In the next lesson you will learn how to add clip art to your slides.

Lesson 11
Adding Graphics to a Slide

In this lesson, you learn how to add PowerPoint clip art to your presentations and how to add images from other sources.

Introducing the Insert Clip Art Task Pane

With the introduction of the task pane in Office XP, accessing clip art and other graphics for use on your PowerPoint slides has changed dramatically from earlier versions of Office. The Insert Clip Art task pane provides you with a search engine that you can use to search for clip art, photographs, movies, and sounds that are stored on your computer. You also can search for clip art and other items using Microsoft's online clip library. (You must be connected to the Internet when using PowerPoint to access the Microsoft online library.)

Figure 11.1 shows the Insert Clip Art task pane. You can use this task pane to search for and insert images onto your slides, or you can take advantage of slides that use a layout that contains a placeholder for images and clip art.

You learn about using the Clip Art task pane and slide layouts that provide image placeholders in this lesson. In Lesson 12, "Adding Sounds and Movies to a Slide," you take a look at using the Clip Art task pane to add movies and slides to your PowerPoint slides.

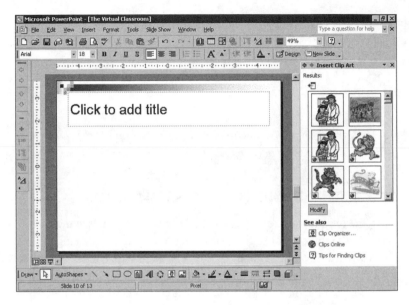

FIGURE 11.1
The Insert Clip Art task pane manages pictures, motion clips, and sounds—all in one convenient place.

PLAIN ENGLISH

> **Clip Art**   A collection of previously created images or pictures that you can place on a slide. Microsoft Office provides clip art and other media types, such as movies and sounds.

You can open the Clip Art task pane in any of these ways:

- Click the **Insert Clip Art** button on the Drawing toolbar.

- Select the **Insert** menu, point at **Picture**, and then choose **Clip Art**.

- Open the task pane, click the task pane drop-down arrow, and then select **Insert Clip Art** to switch to the Insert Clip Art task pane.

When you use the Insert Clip Art task pane, you search for images by keywords. In the following sections, you take a look at inserting clip art from the task pane and learn how you can insert clip art using some of the slide layouts (that provide a clip art placeholder on the slide).

TIP

Clip Organizer Scan The first time you open the Insert Clip Art task pane, PowerPoint prompts you to allow the Clip Organizer (which is discussed later in the lesson) to search your hard drive. Clip Organizer then creates category folders and image indexes from the clip art and images that it finds there. Click **Yes** to allow this process to take place.

INSERTING AN IMAGE FROM THE TASK PANE

As previously mentioned, the Insert Clip Art task pane allows you to search for clip art files using keywords. If you wanted to search for clip art of cats, you would search for the word "cats." To insert a piece of the clip art using the task pane, follow these steps:

1. Select the slide on which you want to place the image so that it appears in the Slide pane.

2. Select **Insert**, point at **Picture**, and then select **Clip Art**. The Insert Clip Art task pane appears.

3. Type keywords into the Search Text box in the task pane that will be used to find your clip art images.

4. Click the **Search** button. Images that match your search criteria appear in the task pane as thumbnails.

5. In the Results list, locate the image that you want to place on the slide. Then click the image, and the clip art is placed on the slidementioned, (see Figure 11.2).

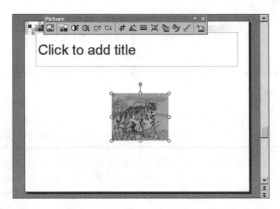

FIGURE 11.2
Click the clip art thumbnail to place the image onto the current slide.

You can use the sizing handles on the image to size the clip art box. Or you can drag the clip art box to a new location on the slide.

INSERTING AN IMAGE FROM AN IMAGE BOX

Another way you can add clip art images to a slide in your presentation is to create the slide using a slide format that supplies a clip art placeholder box on the slide. These slide layout types are called content layouts because they make it easy to insert objects such as clip art, charts, and other items onto a slide. You then can use the object placeholder on the slide to access the clip art library and insert a particular image onto the slide.

Follow these steps:

1. Create a new slide or select the slide to which you want to assign a layout that contains a clip art placeholder box.

2. Open the task pane (**View**, **Task Pane**), and then click the task pane drop-down menu and select **Slide Layout** (the Slide Layout task pane automatically opens if you've just created a new slide).

3. Scroll down through the layouts provided until you locate either the Content layout or the Text and Content layout. Both of these layout categories provide slide layouts that contain object placeholders or object placeholders and text boxes, respectively.

4. Select the layout that best suits the purpose of your slide (see Figure 11.3).

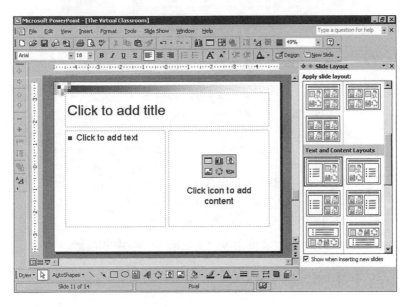

FIGURE 11.3
Select a slide layout that contains an object placeholder.

5. The slide layout you choose provides you with a placeholder box that contains icons for tables, charts, clip art, and other objects. Click the **Insert Clip Art** icon in the placeholder box. The Select Picture dialog box appears (see Figure 11.4).

FIGURE 11.4
The Select Picture dialog box enables you to scroll through or search through the entire clip art and image library on your computer.

6. Scroll down through the list of clip art and other images to find a particular image (the list will be lengthy because it includes all the Office Clip Art and any other images that were located on your computer when the Clip Organizer cataloged the images on your computer).

7. You can search for particular images by keyword. Type the search criteria into the Search Text box, and then click **Search**. Images that match the search criteria appear in the Select Picture dialog box.

8. Click the picture thumbnail that you want to place on the slide. Then click **OK**.

PowerPoint places the image on the slide in the object placeholder box. You can size the box or move it on the slide.

INSERTING A CLIP FROM A FILE

If you have an image stored on your computer that you would like to place on a slide, you can insert the picture directly from the file. This means that you don't have to use the Insert Clip Art task pane to search for and then insert the image.

To place a graphical image on a slide directly from a file, follow these steps:

1. Select the slide on which the image will be placed.

2. Select the **Insert** menu, point at **Picture**, and then select **From File**. The Insert Picture dialog box appears (see Figure 11.5).

FIGURE 11.5
Use the Insert Picture dialog box to place images on a slide.

3. Select the picture you want to use. You can view all the picture files in a particular location as thumbnails. Select the **Views** button, and then select **Thumbnails** on the menu that appears.

4. Click **Insert** to place the image on the slide.

If the picture is too big or too small, you can drag the selection handles (the small squares) around the edge of the image to resize it. Hold down the **Shift** key to proportionally resize the image (this maintains the height/width ratio of the image so that you cannot stretch or distort it). See Lesson 13, "Working with PowerPoint Objects," for more details about resizing and cropping images and other objects on a slide.

TIP

> **Link It Up**   You can link a graphic to the presentation so that, whenever the original changes, the version in the presentation changes, too. Just open the drop-down list on the **Insert** button in the Insert Picture dialog box (refer to Figure 11.5) and choose **Link to File**.

MANAGING IMAGES IN THE CLIP ORGANIZER

Occasionally, you might want to add or delete clip art images from folders on your computer. Managing images is accomplished using the Clip Organizer. When you install Microsoft PowerPoint or Microsoft Office XP (using the default installation), a fairly large library of clip art is placed on your hard drive in different category folders. You can manage these clip art images and other images on your computer, such as scanned images or pictures from a digital camera. To open the Clip Organizer, follow these steps:

1. With the Insert Clip Art task pane open in the PowerPoint window, click the **Clip Organizer** link near the bottom of the task pane to open the Clip Organizer.

2. To view the clip art categories PowerPoint (or Office) has provided, click the plus sign (+) to the left of the Office Collections folder in the Collection list (this folder is located on the left side of the Clip Organizer window). Category folders such as Academic, Agriculture, and so on will appear in the Collection list.

3. Click one of the category folders to view the clip art that it holds (for example, click **Food**). The clip art in that category folder appears in the Clip Organizer window (see Figure 11.6).

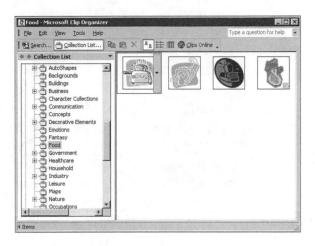

FIGURE 11.6
Use the Clip Organizer to manage your clip art and image files.

Not only does the Clip Organizer allow you to browse the various clip
art and other images on your computer, it allows you to copy, delete,
or move images. For example, if you find an image you no longer
want to store on your computer, select the image in the Clip Organizer
window and press **Delete**. A dialog box appears, letting you know that
this image will be removed from all collections on the computer. Click
OK to delete the image.

You also can use the Clip Organizer to copy or move clip art images
from a location on your hard drive to one of the clip art collections.
Locate the images you want to move or copy to a particular collection,
and then select them.

To move the images to a collection, Select the **Edit** menu, and then
Move to Collection. The Move to Collection dialog box appears (see
Figure 11.7). Select a location in the dialog box and click **OK** to move
the selected image or images.

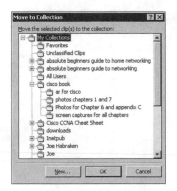

FIGURE 11.7
You can move images from one location to another using the Clip Organizer.

You also can copy images to a new location using the Copy to Collection command. Select the images in a particular folder on your computer using the Clip Organizer window. Select the **Edit** menu and then **Copy to Collection**. Select a location in the Copy to Collection dialog box where you would like to place copies of the images, and then click **OK**.

In this lesson, you learned how to add clip art and other images to your slides. In the next lesson, you learn how to add sounds and videos to your PowerPoint slides.

LESSON 12
Adding Sounds and Movies to a Slide

In this lesson, you learn how to add sound and video clips to a PowerPoint presentation.

WORKING WITH SOUNDS AND MOVIES

A great way to add some interest to your PowerPoint presentations is to add sounds and movies to your slides. Sounds enable you to emphasize certain slides, and movie animations can add humor and style to your presentations. Next, you take a look at adding sounds and then adding movie animations to your slides.

INCLUDING SOUNDS IN A PRESENTATION

Sounds can be used to add emphasis to information on slides or to add some auditory interest to your presentation. You can place sound files on your slides in two different ways:

- You can insert a sound clip as an icon on a slide. When you click the icon, the sound plays.

- You can assign a sound to another object on a slide so that the sound plays when you click the object. For example, you could assign a sound to an image. When you click the image, the sound plays (sounds added to PowerPoint animations play when the animation plays).

INSERTING A SOUND ONTO A SLIDE

To insert a sound clip as an object onto a slide, you can either use the Insert Clip Art task pane or insert the sound as a file. The Clip Art task pane can provide you only with sound files that have been included in the Office clip art library or sound files that you have added to your collection using the Clip Organizer (which is discussed in the previous lesson). Any sound file that you have recorded or otherwise acquired can be inserted as a file.

To insert a sound clip from the Clip Art task pane, follow these steps:

1. Select the slide on which you will place the sound, so that it appears in the Slide pane.

2. Select **Insert**, point at **Movies and Sounds**, and then select **Sound from Media Gallery**. The Insert Clip Art task pane appears with a list of sound files.

3. To preview a particular sound file, point at the file and click the menu arrow that appears. Select **Preview/Properties** from the menu. The Preview/Properties dialog box for that sound file appears (see Figure 12.1).

FIGURE 12.1
Preview a sound clip before placing it onto a slide.

4. To play the sound, click the **Play** button on the left side of the dialog box. When you have finished previewing a sound file, click **Close** to close the Preview/Properties dialog box.

5. When you are ready to insert a sound file onto the slide, click the sound file on the task pane.

6. A dialog box opens, asking you whether you want the sound to play automatically when you run the slide show. Click **Yes** to have the sound played automatically. Click **No** to set up the sound so that you will have to click it during the slide show to play the sound.

Regardless of whether you choose to have PowerPoint play the sound automatically, it appears as a sound icon on the slide.

If you have recorded a sound file or have acquired a sound file that you want to use on a slide without using the Insert Clip Art task pane, you can insert it as a file. To insert a sound clip from a file, follow these steps:

1. Choose the **Insert** menu, point at **Movies and Sounds**, and then choose **Sound from File**.

2. In the Insert Sound dialog box, navigate to the drive and folder containing the sound you want to use (see Figure 12.2).

3. Select the sound clip and click **OK**.

4. A dialog box opens, asking you whether you want the sound to play automatically when you run the slide show. As with the earlier steps, you can click **Yes** to have the sound played automatically or **No** to set up the sound so that you will have to click it during the slide show to play the sound.

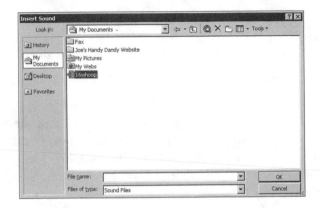

FIGURE 12.2
Choose the sound clip you want to include on your slide.

Like before, the sound file appears on the slide as a sound icon. If you want to play the sound file on the slide, right-click the sound icon and select **Play Sound** from the shortcut menu.

ASSOCIATING A SOUND WITH ANOTHER OBJECT ON THE SLIDE

If you want to avoid having a sound icon on your slide, you can associate the sound with some other object already on the slide, such as a graphic. To do so, follow these steps:

1. Right-click the object (such as a clip art image) to which you want to assign the sound.

2. Choose **Action Settings** from the shortcut menu. The Actions Settings dialog box appears.

3. If you want the sound to play when the object is pointed at, click the **Mouse Over** tab. Otherwise, click the **Mouse Click** tab. The Mouse Click option requires that the sound icon be clicked on for the sound to play.

4. Click the **Play Sound** check box. A drop-down list of sounds becomes available (see Figure 12.3).

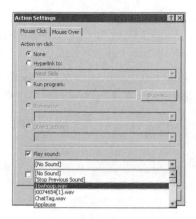

FIGURE 12.3
Choose a sound to be associated with the object.

5. Open the **Play Sound** drop-down list and choose the sound you want.

   If the sound you want is not on the list, choose **Other Sound** and locate the sound using the Add Sound dialog box that appears. Select the sound from there, and click **OK**.

6. When you have chosen the sound you want, click **OK** to close the Action Settings dialog box.

Now, when you are giving the presentation, you can play the sound by either clicking or pointing at the object (depending on how you configured the sound to play). To test this, jump to the Slide Show view (Select the **View** menu and click **Slide Show**) and try it out. Press **Esc** to return to the Normal view when you are finished testing the sound file.

PLACING A MOVIE ONTO A SLIDE

The procedure for placing a movie onto a slide is very much the same as that for a sound. You can place a movie using the Insert Clip Art task pane or from a file. You will find that the task pane Clip Gallery provides several movies that can be used to add interest to your slides. To insert a movie onto a slide, follow these steps:

1. Choose the **Insert** menu, point at **Movies and Sounds**, and then select **Movies from Clip Gallery**.

2. Scroll through the movies listed on the Insert Clip Art task pane.

3. Point at a movie clip you want to preview. Click the menu arrow that appears and select **Preview/Properties**. The Preview Properties dialog box for the movie appears.

4. PowerPoint previews the movie on the left side of the dialog box (see Figure 12.4). If you want to place a caption onto the movie clip, click in the **Caption** box below the Preview pane and type a caption.

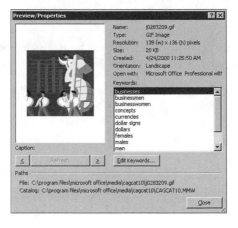

FIGURE 12.4
Preview a movie in the Preview/Properties dialog box.

5. Click **Close** to close the Preview/Properties dialog box. To insert the movie into your slide, click the movie in the task pane.

After the movie icon is in place on your slide, you can size the movie box using the usual sizing handles or move it to another position on the slide. If you want to test view the movie on the slide, jump to the Slide Show view (select the **View** menu and then click **Slide Show**) and try it out. Press **Esc** to return to the Normal view when you are finished testing the movie.

PLAIN ENGLISH

Clip Gallery Movies Really Aren't Movies   The clip gallery movies provided by Microsoft Office are really just animations. They are designed to play automatically when the slide containing the image is opened during a slide show.

You can also place actual videos on a slide as a file. This enables you to place video captures that you have created or video files from other sources. Follow these steps:

1. Choose the **Insert** menu, point at **Movies and Sounds**, and then choose **Movie from File**.

2. In the Insert Sound dialog box that appears, navigate to the drive and folder containing the movie file you want to use.

3. Select the file and click **OK** to place it on the slide.

4. A dialog box appears (see Figure 12.5) that allows you to have the movie play when the slide appears in the slide show. Click **Yes**. To require that you click the movie's icon to make it play during the slide show, click **No**.

FIGURE 12.5
You can choose how the movie will be handled during the slide show.

After you make your selection in step 4, PowerPoint places the movie onto the slide. To preview the video file on the slide, right-click the video icon and select **Play Movie**.

In this lesson, you learned how to place sounds and movies in your presentation for great multimedia effects. In the next lesson, you learn how to select objects; work with object layers; and cut, copy, and paste objects.

Lesson 13

Working with PowerPoint Objects

In this lesson, you learn how to manipulate objects on your slides, such as clip art and other items, to create impressive presentations.

Selecting Objects

In the previous two lessons, you learned about inserting clip art, image files, sound files, and movie files onto the slides of your PowerPoint presentation. Any type of special content that you place on a slide is called an *object*. In addition to the object types just listed, objects could also be items from other Office applications. For example, you could create an object on a slide that actually is an Excel worksheet or chart (for more about sharing information between Office applications see Lesson 14, "Using Microsoft Office Objects in Presentations."

After you select an object, you can do all kinds of things to it, such as copying, moving, deleting, or resizing it. The following is a review of ways you can select objects on a PowerPoint slide:

- To select a single object, click it. (If you click text, a frame appears around the text. Click the frame to select the text object.)

- To select more than one object, hold down the **Ctrl** or **Shift** key while clicking each object. Handles appear around the selected objects, as shown in Figure 13.1 (this temporarily groups the objects so that you can move them all simultaneously on the slide).

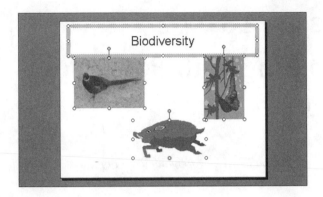

FIGURE 13.1
You can select multiple objects on a slide.

- To deselect selected objects, click anywhere outside the selected object or objects.

TIP

> **Select Objects Tool**   Use the Select Objects tool on the Drawing toolbar to drag a selection box around several objects you want to select. When you release the mouse button, PowerPoint selects all the objects inside the box.

WORKING WITH LAYERS OF OBJECTS

As you place objects onscreen, they might start to overlap, creating layers of objects where the lower layers are often difficult or impossible to select. To move objects in layers, perform the following steps:

1. Click the object you want to move up or down in the stack. If the Drawing toolbar is not available in the PowerPoint window, right-click on any toolbar and select **Drawing** from the menu that appears.

2. Click the **Draw** button on the Drawing toolbar to open the Draw menu, and select **Order**, as shown in Figure 13.2.

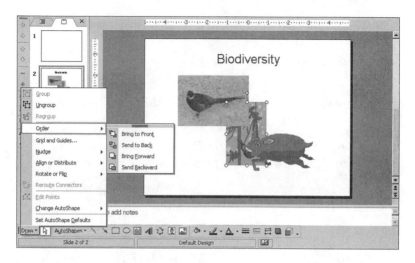

FIGURE 13.2
Use the Draw menu on the Drawing toolbar to change the layer on which a graphic appears on your slide.

3. Select one of the following options:

- **Bring to Front**—Brings the object to the top of the stack.

- **Send to Back**—Sends the object to the bottom of the stack.

- **Bring Forward**—Brings the object up one layer.

- **Send Backward**—Sends the object back one layer.

GROUPING AND UNGROUPING OBJECTS

Each object on a slide, including text boxes, is an individual object. However, sometimes you want two or more objects to act as a group. For example, you might want to make the lines of several objects the same thickness or group several objects so that they can easily be moved together on the slide. If you want to treat two or more objects as a group, perform the following steps:

1. Select the objects you want to group. Remember, to select more than one object, hold down the **Shift** or **Ctrl** key as you click each one.

2. Click the **Draw** button on the Drawing toolbar to open the Draw menu, and then select **Group**.

3. To ungroup the objects, select any object in the group and select **Draw**, and then choose **Ungroup**.

CUTTING, COPYING, AND PASTING OBJECTS

You can cut, copy, and paste objects onto a slide (or onto another slide) the same as you would normal text. When you cut an object, PowerPoint removes the object from the slide and places it in a temporary holding area called the Office Clipboard. When you copy or cut an object, a copy of the object, or the object itself when you use Cut, is placed on the Office Clipboard. You can place multiple objects onto the Clipboard and paste them as needed onto a slide or slides in your presentation.

To view the Office Clipboard, select **View**, **Task Pane**. Then, on the task pane drop-down menu, select **Clipboard**. Figure 13.3 shows the Clipboard task pane.

FIGURE 13.3
Use the Clipboard to keep track of objects that you have cut or copied.

To cut or copy an object, perform the following steps:

1. Select the object(s) you want to cut, copy, or move.

2. Select the **Edit** menu and then choose **Cut** or **Copy**, or click the **Cut** or **Copy** buttons on the Standard toolbar.

 TIP

> **Right-Click Shortcut**   Right-click a selection to choose **Cut** or **Copy** from the shortcut menu.

3. Display the slide on which you want to paste the cut or copied objects.

4. Select **Edit** and then choose **Paste**, or click the **Paste** button on the Standard toolbar. PowerPoint pastes the objects onto the slide.

TIP

Keyboard Shortcuts   Instead of using the toolbar buttons or the menu, you can press **Ctrl+X** to cut, **Ctrl+C** to copy, and **Ctrl+V** to paste.

To remove an object without placing it on the Clipboard, select the object and press the **Delete** key.

Rotating an Object

When you select an object on a slide, a handle with a green end on it appears at the top center of the object. This is the rotation handle, and it can be used to rotate any object on a slide. The rotation handle enables you to revolve an object around a center point.

To rotate an object, do the following:

1. Click the object you want to rotate.

2. Place the mouse pointer on the object's Rotation handle (the green dot) until the Rotation icon appears.

3. Hold down the mouse button and drag the Rotation handle until the object is in the position you want.

4. Release the mouse button.

The Draw menu (on the Drawing toolbar) also enables you to rotate or flip an object. You can flip an object horizontally left or right or flip the object vertically from top to bottom. To flip an object, click the **Draw** button on the Drawing toolbar, and then point at **Rotate and Flip**. Select either **Flip Horizontal** or **Flip Vertical** from the menu that appears.

TIP

> **Can't Find the Drawing Toolbar?**   If the Drawing toolbar
> does not appear at the bottom of the PowerPoint appli-
> cation window, right-click any visible toolbar and select
> **Drawing**.

RESIZING OBJECTS

You will find that objects such as pictures and clip art are not always
inserted onto a slide in the correct size. You can resize the object by
performing these steps:

1. Select the object to resize. Selection handles appear.

2. Drag one of the following handles (the squares that surround
    the object) until the object is the desired size:

    • Drag a corner handle to change both the height and
      width of an object. PowerPoint retains the object's
      height-to-width ratio.

    • Drag a side, top, or bottom handle to change the height
      or width alone.

    • To keep the original center of the object stationary
      while sizing, hold down the **Ctrl** key while dragging a
      sizing handle.

3. Release the mouse button when you have finished resizing
    the object.

CROPPING A PICTURE

Besides resizing a picture, you can crop it; that is, you can trim a side
or a corner off the picture to remove an element from the picture or
cut off some whitespace. This enables you to clean up the picture
within the object box.

To crop a picture, perform the following steps:

1. Click the picture you want to crop.

2. To crop the picture, you need the Picture toolbar. Right-click any toolbar currently showing in the PowerPoint window and select **Picture**. The Picture toolbar appears.

3. Click the **Crop** button on the Picture toolbar. Cropping handles appear around the picture (see Figure 13.4).

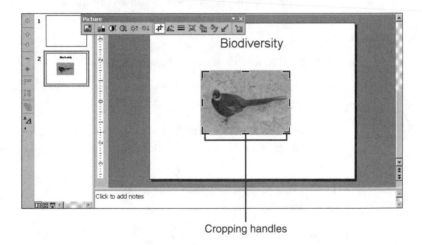

Cropping handles

FIGURE 13.4
Use the cropping handles on the figure to crop portions of the picture.

4. Move the mouse pointer over one of the cropping handles. The mouse pointer becomes the same shape as the cropping handle. (Use a corner handle to crop two sides at once. Use a side, top, or bottom handle to crop only one side.)

5. Hold down the mouse button and drag the pointer until the crop lines are where you want them.

6. Release the mouse button. PowerPoint crops the image.

7. After cropping that image, move or resize the picture as needed.

CAUTION

> **Stop That Crop!**   To undo the cropping of a picture immediately after you crop it, select **Edit** and then choose **Undo Crop Picture**.

In this lesson, you learned how to select, copy, move, rotate, and resize an object on a slide. You also learned how to crop an image. In the next lesson, you learn how to insert objects from other Microsoft applications into PowerPoint presentations.

LESSON 14
Adding Charts to PowerPoint Slides

In this lesson, you learn how to add charts to PowerPoint slides and how to enhance those charts.

USING CHARTS IN PRESENTATIONS

Because your PowerPoint presentations serve the basic purpose of allowing your audience to visualize the subject matter that you are presenting, the use of charts is a great way to visually represent numerical data. Although many people find tables of statistics intimidating, providing a "picture" of the data in a form of a chart will greatly enhance audience understanding of important information as you give your presentation.

PowerPoint provides a Chart feature that enables you to create several different chart types. The following are some of the commonly used chart types:

- **Pie**—Use this chart type to show the relationship among parts of a whole.

- **Bar**—Use this chart type to compare values at a given point in time.

- **Column**—Similar to the bar chart; use this chart type to emphasize the difference between items.

- **Line**—Use this chart type to emphasize trends and the change of values over time.

- **Scatter**—Similar to a line chart; use this chart type to emphasize the difference between two sets of values.

- **Area**—Similar to the line chart; use this chart type to emphasize the amount of change in values over time.

The data represented by the chart is placed in a datasheet that is similar to the worksheets provided by spreadsheet software such as Microsoft Excel. This means that you enter the numerical information that creates the chart in a series of rows and columns. Each block created by the intersection of a row and column is referred to as a *cell*.

PLAIN ENGLISH

> **Cell**—The block created by the intersection of a row and column in the chart datasheet.

The data you place in the datasheet appears on the chart along a particular axis of the chart. A two-dimensional chart has an x-axis (horizontal) and a y-axis (vertical). The x-axis typically contains the text description found in the chart (which would be the column headings found on the datasheet). The y-axis typically reflects the values of the bars, lines, or plot points. The y-axis information would the numerical data that you place under each column heading in the datasheet.

PLAIN ENGLISH

> **Axis**—One side of a chart. A two-dimensional chart has an x-axis (horizontal) and a y-axis (vertical).

Not only will a chart contain an x- and y-axis; it also will contain a legend. The legend defines the separate data series of a chart. For example, the legend for a pie chart shows what each piece of the pie represents. The legend information typically would be the same as the row headings that you place in the datasheet.

PLAIN ENGLISH

Legend—Defines the separate numerical series of a chart. For example, the legend for a column chart shows what each column in the chart represents.

You can add a chart to an existing slide using the Chart command on the Insert menu. You also can place a chart on a slide by creating a new slide that uses a slide layout that includes a chart object. Let's take a look at both these possibilities, and then we can look at some ways in which you can enhance a chart to maximum its visual impact in your PowerPoint presentation.

TIP

Using Charts From Excel   PowerPoint enables you to create charts by entering information into a datasheet, but you also can opt to paste charts from Excel onto a PowerPoint slide. This certainly makes sense if you have already entered the data in an Excel worksheet and created a chart. Open Excel and PowerPoint and use the Copy and Paste commands to place a copy of the Excel chart on any PowerPoint slide. For information about copying objects, see Lesson 13, "Working with PowerPoint Objects."

INSERTING A CHART ON AN EXISTING SLIDE

PowerPoint enables you to insert a chart on any existing slide. When the chart appears on the slide, it will be in the default format, which is a column chart (a vertical bar chart). We will discuss how to change the chart type later in this lesson.

To insert a chart on a slide, follow these steps:

1. Open the slide on which you will place the chart.

2. Select the **Insert** menu, and then select **Chart**. The chart will appear on the slide, and the chart's datasheet also will appear in the PowerPoint window, as shown in Figure 14.1.

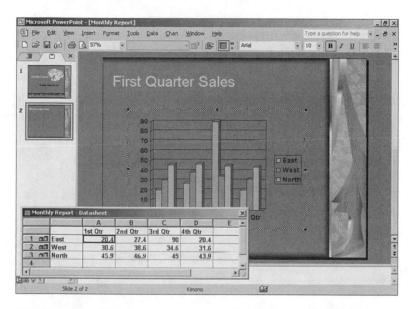

FIGURE 14.1
The chart and the chart's datasheet appear in the PowerPoint window.

3. To establish the x-axis text labels for the chart, click in the cell that currently contains the text **1st Qtr**. Type the new column heading that you will use for your chart. For example, if you are doing a summary of the first quarter's profit for your business, type **January**.

4. Press the **Tab** key to move to the next cell (or click in the cell using the mouse) and change the column heading as needed. If you need to delete a row or column of the default information on the datasheet, click the row number or column letter to select that row or column, respectively. Then, press the **Delete** key to clear the data.

5. Change the row headings to reflect the information you want to place on the chart's legend. Figure 14.2 shows a modified datasheet for a chart.

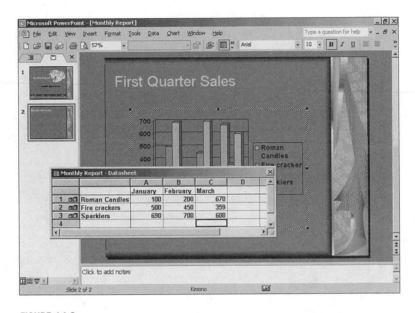

FIGURE 14.2
Modify the datasheet information to create your chart.

6. When you have finished entering the data for the chart, you can close the datasheet by clicking its **Close** button.

 TIP

> **Widening Datasheet Columns**   When you are adding text descriptions to your column headings in the datasheet, you might find that the headings are cut off. To widen the columns, place the mouse on the dividing line between the columns and use the sizing tool that appears to resize the column width so that it accommodates the text.

As already mentioned, the default chart type is a column chart. We will take a look at how you change the chart type in a moment.

CREATING A NEW SLIDE CONTAINING A CHART

An alternative to inserting a chart in an existing slide is to create a new slide that contains a placeholder for a chart. PowerPoint provides three different slide layouts that contain a chart placeholder object. You can create a slide that contains a title, bulleted list, and chart in two variations, with either the chart on the left or right of the slide. A third alternative provides a slide layout that contains a title and a chart only.

To create a new slide containing a chart, follow these steps:

1. Select the slide in the Slides pane (or Outline pane) that will provide the position in the presentation for the new slide (the new slide will be inserted after the selected slide).

2. Select the **Insert** menu, and then select **New Slide**. The New slide will appear in the presentation and open in the Slide view. The Slide Layout task pane also will open in the PowerPoint window.

3. Scroll down through the layouts provided in the task pane and select a slide layout that contains a chart placeholder (the layout icon will contain an image of a column chart).

4. The Chart layout will be changed to a slide that contains a chart (see Figure 14.3).

5. Double-click on the chart placeholder on the slide (it says "Double click to add chart").

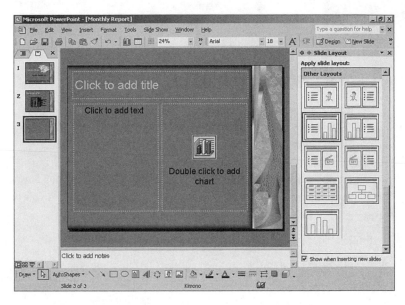

FIGURE 14.3
Create a new slide that contains a chart placeholder.

6. The datasheet for the chart will appear. Enter your data and row and column headings for the chart as discussed in the previous section.

7. Close the datasheet when you have finished entering your data.

SELECTING THE CHART TYPE

After you have created a chart on a slide, either by inserting the chart or by creating a new slide containing a chart (and filled in your data on the datasheet), you will want to be able to select the chart type that is used. As mentioned in the opening of this lesson, several different chart types are available.

To select the chart type, follow these steps:

1. Be sure the chart is selected on the slide.

2. Select the **Chart** menu, and then select **Chart Type**. The Chart Type dialog box will appear (see Figure 14.4).

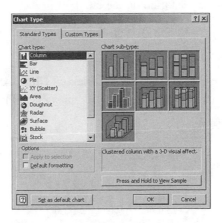

FIGURE 14.4
Use the Chart Type dialog box to specify your chart type.

3. In the Chart type box, select the chart type you wish to use (such as Bar, Line, or Pie).

4. Each chart type will provide several subtypes. Use the subtype box to select the "look" of your chart.

5. (Optional) If you want to view a sample of a particular chart type (and the selected subtype) click and hold the **Press and Hold to View Sample** button.

6. When you have selected the type and subtype for your chart, click **OK**.

You will be returned to your slide and your chart will appear on the slide. If you want to change the chart type, you can select the chart, and then follow the preceding steps to edit the chart type or the subtype.

Modifying the Chart's Attributes

You can change the look of your chart by modifying the chart's border. You can change the color or add a shadow to the chart border. You also can modify the font used on the chart.

To modify the chart, follow these steps:

1. Select the chart on the slide.

2. Select **Format**, and then select **Selected Chart Area**. The Format Chart Area dialog box will appear (see Figure 14.5).

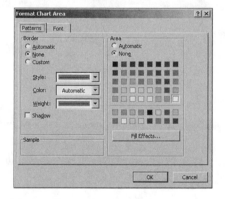

FIGURE 14.5
The Format Chart Area dialog box enables you to change the chart's border and font.

3. On the Patterns tab, select the **Custom** option button. Use the **Style**, **Color**, and **Weight** drop-down boxes to set the various attributes for the chart's border. If you wish to include a shadow on the border, select the **Shadow** check box.

4. To change the font attributes for the chart, click the **Font** tab of the Format Chart Area dialog box.

5. Use the various font attribute drop-down boxes and check boxes to select the custom font settings for the chart (the font attributes provided are the same as those available in the Font dialog box we discussed in Lesson 8, "Adding and Modifying Slide Text").

6. After you have finished making your border and font changes to the chart, click **OK**. You will be returned to the slide.

TIP

You Can Modify the Look of Chart Parts   You can modify the border and font used in specific parts of the chart, such as the legend. Double-click on the particular chart area and the Format dialog box for that particular area will appear. Change the attributes as needed.

In this lesson, you learned how to place a chart on a PowerPoint slide. You also learned how to enhance the chart's attributes, such as the font and border color. In the next lesson, you learn how to add an organizational chart and other diagrams to a PowerPoint slide.

LESSON 15

Adding Organizational Charts to PowerPoint Slides

In this lesson, you learn how to add organizational charts to PowerPoint slides and then edit them.

WORKING WITH ORGANIZATIONAL CHARTS

We have looked at several different object types that you can add to your PowerPoint slides, including clip art, sounds, and charts that display numerical data, such as column charts and pie charts. Another very useful visual object that you can add to your PowerPoint slides is the organizational chart.

Organizational charts often are used to display the report structure for a business or institution. They also can be used to diagram business processes, such as the different steps in a marketing or business plan, and they can be used to create a family tree.

Organizational charts can be added to an existing slide, or you can create a new slide that contains an organizational chart placeholder (when this object is double-clicked, you are provided with the tools that you use to create the chart). When you have an organizational chart on a slide, PowerPoint also provides you with different formatting options for that chart.

INSERTING AN ORGANIZATIONAL CHART ON A SLIDE

You can place an organizational chart on any slide in your presentation. All you need is the appropriate blank space on the slide to accommodate the chart object. To insert an organizational chart onto an existing slide, follow these steps:

1. Display the slide on which you want to place the organizational chart.

2. Select the **Insert** menu, then point at **Picture**, and then select **Organization Chart**. A new chart appears on the slide (as does the Organization Chart toolbar, as shown in Figure 15.1).

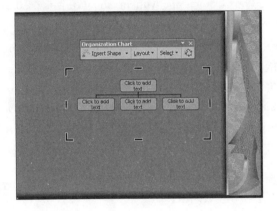

FIGURE 15.1
The organizational chart is placed on the slide.

3. Click on a box in a chart to add text. Enter the appropriate information, such as the name, title, and up to two optional comments about the person in the organization who will appear at that level in the chart. Press **Enter** to start a new line after typing each item. Press **Esc** when you complete the entry for that person.

4. Repeat step 3 for each person or item you want to include in the organizational chart.

5. To add another box to the chart, select a box in the chart to which you want to attach the new box. Then, click the drop-down arrow on the right of the **Insert Shape** button on the Organization Chart toolbar.

6. Select either **Subordinate**, **Coworker**, or **Assistant** from the Insert Shape list. Selecting **Subordinate** will place a new box below (subordinate to) the currently selected box. **Coworker** will place a new box at the same level of the selected box, and **Assistant** will place a new box subordinate to the selected box using a line with an elbow (this is used to differentiate between a subordinate and an assistant).

7. Select the new box that you created and type the appropriate text.

8. When you have finished working with the chart, you can click anywhere on the slide to deselect the chart. This also closes the Organization Chart toolbar.

CREATING A NEW SLIDE CONTAINING AN ORGANIZATIONAL CHART

You can create a new slide that contains a placeholder for an organizational chart. Follow these steps:

1. Select the slide in the Slides pane (or Outline pane) that will provide the position in the presentation for the new slide (the new slide will be inserted after the selected slide).

2. Select the **Insert** menu, and then select **New Slide**. The new slide will appear in the presentation and open in the Slide view. The Slide Layout task pane will also open in the PowerPoint window.

3. Scroll down through the layouts provided in the task pane and select the slide layout that contains Organizational Chart placeholder (it is the second to last layout provided in the task pane). The layout will be assigned to the slide (see Figure 15.2).

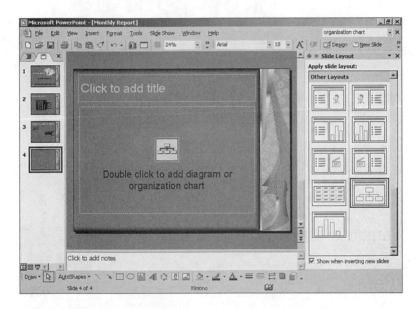

FIGURE 15.2
You can create a new slide that contains an organizational chart.

4. To create the organizational chart, double-click the placeholder box containing the text "Double click to add diagram or organization chart."

5. The Diagram Gallery dialog box will appear (see Figure 15.3). Double-click the **Organizational Chart** button in the dialog box.

FIGURE 15.3
Organizational charts can be placed on a new slide.

6. The organizational chart will be placed on the slide. Place your text entries in the appropriate boxes using the techniques discussed in the previous section.

EDITING AN ORGANIZATIONAL CHART

Editing an organizational chart really is no different than initially creating the chart. Follow these steps:

1. Select the slide containing the chart so that it is displayed in the Slide view.

2. Click on the chart to select it.

3. Select any of the chart boxes to edit the text. You can delete a box by selecting the box and then pressing the **Delete** key.

TIP

Zoom In on Your Chart   As you work on the chart, you can zoom in or out to see more or less of the chart at once. Just open the **View** menu and select a different view percentage.

Another aspect of editing an organizational chart relates to changing the fonts or the color of the chart box borders or background. Before we look at how you change the font for a single box or several selected boxes or work with color attributes, let's look at some strategies for how you can select multiple boxes in a chart:

- To select a single box, click it.

- To select more than one box, hold down the **Shift** key while clicking on each box.

- To select all the boxes at a particular level, select the **Select** drop-down arrow on the Organization Chart toolbar, and then select **Level**.

- To select all the assistants for a selected box, select the **Select** drop-down arrow on the Organization Chart toolbar, and then select **Assistants**.

After you select a box or boxes you can change the font, line, or color attributes for that box or boxes. For example, to change the font for selected boxes, select the **Format** menu and then select **Font**. You then can use the Font dialog box to make any changes to the font for the selected boxes (you would use the Font dialog box just as you would to change regular text on a slide, as discussed in Lesson 8, "Adding and Modifying Slide Text").

FORMATTING BOX LINES AND FILL COLORS

You also might want to change the attributes for a box or boxes in an organizational chart, such as the line style or the fill color. Follow these steps:

1. Select the boxes you want to format (as discussed in the previous section).

2. Select the **Format** menu, and then select **AutoShape**. The Format AutoShape dialog box appears (see Figure 15.4).

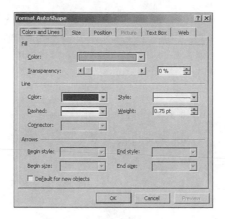

FIGURE 15.4
You can change the border line attributes and the fill color for boxes in the chart.

3. To change the fill color for the box or boxes, click the **Color** drop-down box in the Fill area of the dialog box. Select a new color from the color palette that appears.

4. If you wish to increase the transparency of the box or boxes, move the **Transparency** slider bar to the right (the greater the transparency percentage, the lighter the fill color becomes).

5. To change the line color, style, or weight use the appropriate drop-down box in the **Line** area of the dialog box.

6. When you have finished changing the fill color or the line settings, click **OK** to close the dialog box and return to the slide.

TIP

> **Formatting Connecting Lines**   You can change the line
> style and color of the connecting lines on your organiza-
> tional chart. Select a connecting line or lines (to select
> multiple lines hold down the **Shift** key). Then, right-click
> on the selected lines and select **Format AutoShape** on the
> shortcut menu that appears. The Format AutoShape dia-
> log box will open; it can be used to change the format-
> ting for the selected connecting lines.

CHANGING THE ORGANIZATIONAL CHART STYLE

PowerPoint provides several different styles for your organizational
charts. These styles provide different color schemes, box types, and
even 3-D effects.

To change the style for your chart, follow these steps:

1. Select the organizational chart on the slide.

2. Click the **AutoFormat** button on the Organization Chart tool-
    bar. The Organization Chart Style Gallery dialog box appears
    (see Figure 15.5).

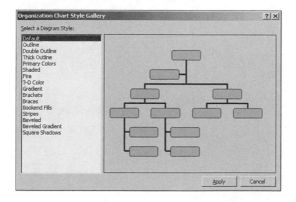

FIGURE 15.5
*You can change the overall style of the chart using the Organization Chart Style
Gallery.*

3. Select one of the styles provided. A preview is provided on the right side of the dialog box.

4. When you have found the style you wish to use for your chart, click the **Apply** button.

The dialog box will close and the style will be applied to your organizational chart.

In this lesson, you learned how to place an organizational chart on a PowerPoint slide. You also learned how to edit a chart. In the next lesson, you learn how to present your slideshow onscreen.

LESSON 16
Presenting an Onscreen Slide Show

In this lesson, you learn how to view a slide show onscreen, how to make basic movements within a presentation, and how to set show options. You also learn how to create a self-running show with timings and how to work with slide transitions.

VIEWING AN ONSCREEN SLIDE SHOW

Before you show your presentation to an audience, you should run through it several times on your own computer, checking that all the slides are in the right order and that the timings and transitions between the slides work correctly. This also enables you to fine-tune any monologue you might have to give as you show the slides so that what you are saying at any point in the presentation is synchronized with the slide that is being shown at that moment.

You can preview a slide show at any time; follow these steps:

1. Open the presentation you want to view.

2. Choose the **Slide Show** menu and choose **View Show**. The first slide in the presentation appears full screen (see Figure 16.1).

FIGURE 16.1
When you run your slide show, the entire screen is used to display the slides.

3. To display the next or the previous slide, do one of the following:

   • To display the next slide, click the left mouse button, press the **Page Down** key, or press the right-arrow or down-arrow key.

   • To display the previous slide, click the right mouse button, press the **Page Up** key, or press the left-arrow or up-arrow key.

4. When you have finished running the slide show, press the **Esc** key.

TIP

> **Start the Show!**   You also can start a slide show by
> clicking the **Slide Show** button in the bottom-left corner
> of the presentation window or by pressing **F5**.

SETTING SLIDE ANIMATION SCHEMES

After running the slide show a few times, you might find that the presentation doesn't really provide the visual impact that you had hoped. Even though you have designed your slides well and created slides that include images and movies, you are still looking for something with a more "artsy" feel. A great way to add visual impact to the presentation is to assign an animation scheme to a slide or slides in the presentation.

An animation scheme controls how the text in the text boxes on the slide appear or materialize on the slide during the presentation. For example, you can select a slide animation scheme called Bounce, where the various text on the slide "bounces" onto the slide when it appears onscreen during the slide show.

PLAIN ENGLISH

> **Animation Scheme**   A scheme that controls how objects
> materialize onto the slide during the slide show.

PowerPoint provides three categories of animation schemes that you can assign to a slide: Subtle, Moderate, and Exciting. Each of these categories provides several animation schemes. The great thing about the animation schemes is that you can assign them to a slide or slides and then try them out in the Normal view. If you don't like the animation scheme, you can select another.

To assign an animation scheme to a slide in the presentation, follow these steps:

1. Select the slide to which you will assign the animation scheme so that it appears in the Slide pane in the Normal view.

2. Select the **Slide Show** menu and select **Animation Schemes**. The Animation Schemes list appears in the Slide Design task pane on the right side of the PowerPoint window (see Figure 16.2).

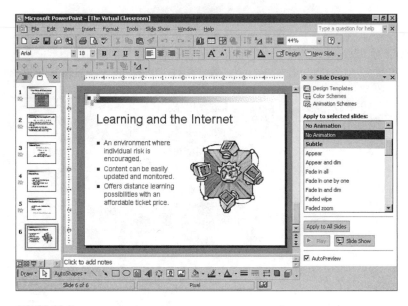

FIGURE 16.2
The task pane houses the animation schemes that you can assign to the slides in your presentation.

3. Scroll through the list of animation schemes. When you find a scheme that you want to try, select the scheme in the list box.

4. To try the scheme, click the **Play** button in the task pane.

5. If you don't like the scheme, select another.

6. If you find a scheme that you would like to apply to all the slides in the presentation, click the **Apply to All Slides** button.

TIP

> **Assign Animation Schemes to Selected Slides**   You can select several slides in the Slide Sorter view and then use the Slide Design task pane to assign the same animation scheme to all the selected slides.

SETTING UP A SELF-RUNNING SHOW

In a self-running show, the slide show runs itself. Each slide advances after a specified period of time. This allows you to concentrate on the narrative aspects of the presentation as you use the slide show for a speech or classroom presentation. For a self-running show, you must set timings. You can set the same timing for all slides (for example, a 20-second delay between each slide), or you can set a separate timing for each slide individually.

When you set up a self-running show, you also can select different slide transitions. A slide transition is a special effect that is executed when the slide appears during the slide show. For example, you can have a slide dissolve onto the screen, or you can have the slide appear on the screen using a checkerboard effect.

To configure the show to use timings and transitions, follow these steps:

1. Open the presentation you want to view.

2. Select the slide to which you would like to apply a timing or transition so that it appears in the Slides pane in the Normal view.

3. Select **Slide Show** and click **Slide Transition**. The Slide Transition task pane opens containing controls for the type of transition you want to use, the speed with which that transition executes, and the length of time the slide should remain onscreen (see Figure 16.3).

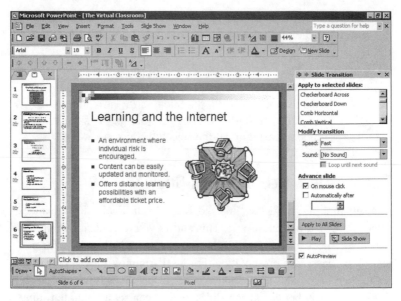

FIGURE 16.3
The Slide Transition task pane houses the controls necessary for tailoring the way a slide transitions onto the screen during a presentation.

4. To select a transition for the slide, select one of the transitions supplied in the Apply to Selected Slides box.

5. To test the transition, click the **Play** button.

6. If you want to change the speed of the transition, click the Speed drop-down list and select **Slow**, **Medium**, or **Fast** (Fast is the default).

7. (Optional) If you want to select a sound to accompany the slide transition (such as Applause, Drum Roll, or Laser), click the **Sound** drop-down list and select one of the supplied sounds.

8. To set the timing for the slide in the Advance Slide section of the task pane, click the **Automatically After** check box. Use the click box below the check box to enter the number of seconds for the slide's automatic timing.

9. If you want to apply the selected transition and the timing to all the slides in the presentation, click the **Apply to All Slides** button.

CAUTION

> **My Slides Don't Advance Using the Timings**   If you find when you run the slide show that the slides don't advance using the timings that you have set, select **Slide Show**, **Set Up Show**. In the Set Up Show dialog box, be sure that the **Using Timings, If Present** option button is selected. Then click **OK**.

When you run the slide show, the slides advance according to the timings that you have set. The slides also use any transitions that you have selected for them. Take the time to run the slide show several times so that you can gauge whether the transitions and timings work well. Remember that the slide must be onscreen long enough for your audience to read and understand the text on the slide.

TIP

> **Assign Transitions and Timings to Selected Slides**   You can select several slides in the Slide Sorter view and then use the Slide Transition task pane to assign the same transition and/or timing to the selected slides.

CAUTION

> **Don't Get Too Fancy!**   If you are going to use slide transitions and animation schemes on each and every slide, you might find that your slide show is becoming "too exciting," like a film with too many explosions, car chases, and other special effects. Viewers of the slide show likely will have trouble concentrating on the text on the slides if too many things are going on at once. Remember, everything in moderation.

USING THE SLIDE SHOW MENU TOOLS

PowerPoint also provides some other features that you will find very useful when you are running your slide show. For example, you can turn the mouse pointer into a pen that enables you to draw on a particular slide, enabling you to quickly emphasize a particular point visually. A Meeting Minder feature enables you to take notes during the actual presentation, which is a great way to record audience questions or comments concerning the presentation as you actually show it.

These tools are found on a menu that you can access during a slide show by right-clicking the screen. Figure 16.4 shows the menu. Three of the most useful tools are discussed in the following sections of this lesson.

FIGURE 16.4
You can access the pen and other tools, such as your Speaker Notes, from the menu on the Slide Show screen.

DRAWING WITH THE PEN

An extremely useful tool is the pen, which enables you to draw on a particular slide. This is great for highlighting information on a slide to emphasize a particular point.

To use the pen during the slide show, follow these steps:

1. With the slide show running, right-click anywhere on the screen. The Slide Show menu appears.

2. Point at **Pointer Options** on the menu, and then choose **Pen**. The mouse pointer becomes a pen.

3. Press the left mouse button and draw on the slide as needed (see Figure 16.5).

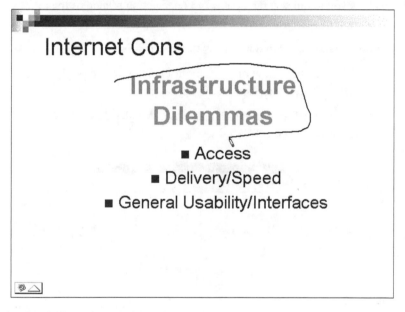

FIGURE 16.5
The pen provides you with an easy way to highlight a particular item on a slide.

4. After you've finished working with the pen, you can return to the arrow pointer. Right-click on the screen, point at **Pointer Options** on the menu, and then select **Arrow**. You now can use the mouse to advance to the next slide.

You also can choose the pen color that you use to draw on the slides. This option is available on the Slide Show menu (point at **Pointer Options**, point at **Pen Color**, and then select the pen color you want to use from the cascading menu).

TAKING NOTES WITH THE MEETING MINDER

Another useful tool that you can take advantage of while showing your slide presentation is the Meeting Minder. The Meeting Minder enables you to quickly take notes or create action related to the discussion or to audience comments made during your presentation.

To use the Meeting Minder, follow these steps:

1. With the slide show running, right-click anywhere on the screen. The Slide Show menu appears.

2. Click **Meeting Minder**. The Meeting Minder dialog box opens (see Figure 16.6.)

FIGURE 16.6
The Meeting Minder makes it easy for you to record notes or a task related to your presentation.

3. Type your notes onto the **Meeting Minutes** tab of the dialog box.

4. If you want to create an action item, click the **Action Items** tab on the dialog box. Type a description into the **Description** box, and type the name of the person who will work on

the item into the **Assigned To** box. After filling in this information, click the **Add** button to add the item to the Action
Items list on the tab.

5. When you have finished adding notes or creating action items
   related to the slide presentation, click the **OK** button to close
   the dialog box.

FINDING A PARTICULAR SLIDE DURING THE SHOW

As you reach the end of a presentation, you might be asked to reshow
a particular slide or subset of slides that you included in your slide
show. The easiest way to go to a particular slide when you are in the
Slide Show view is by using the Slide Navigator. The Slide Navigator
lists all the slides in the current slide show.

To use the Slide Navigator, follow these steps:

1. With the slide show running, right-click anywhere on the
   screen. The Slide Show menu appears.

2. Point at **Go** and then click **Slide Navigator**. The Slide
   Navigator dialog box opens.

3. To move to a particular slide, click the slide's title in the
   Slide Navigator's slide list and then click **Go To**. PowerPoint
   takes you to the selected slide.

ADDING ACTION BUTTONS TO USER-INTERACTIVE SHOWS

You may create slide show presentations that will be played on a computer where your audience actually interacts with the slide show (for
example, a computer at a trade show that tells potential customers
about your company). This means that you need to give the audience
some means of controlling the show. You can simply provide access to
a keyboard and/or mouse and let the user control the show in the same
way you learned earlier in this lesson, or you can provide action buttons onscreen that make it easy to jump to specific slides.

Action buttons are like controls on an audio CD player; they enable you to jump to any slide quickly, to go backward, to go forward, or even to stop the presentation.

 TIP

> **The Same Controls on All Slides?**   If you want to add the same action buttons to all slides in the presentation, add the action buttons to the Slide Master. To display the Slide Master, select **View**, point at **Master**, and then choose **Slide Master**.

To add an action button to a slide, follow these steps:

1. Display the slide in Normal view.

2. Select **Slide Show**, point at **Action Buttons**, and pick a button from the palette that appears. For example, if you want to create a button that advances to the next slide, you might choose the button with the arrow pointing to the right.

 TIP

> **Which Button Should I Choose?**   Consider the action that you want the button to perform, and then pick a button picture that matches it well. To change the button picture, you must delete the button and create a new one.

3. Your mouse pointer turns into a crosshair. Drag to draw a box on the slide where you want the button to appear. (You can resize it later if you want.) PowerPoint draws the button on the slide and opens the Action Settings dialog box (see Figure 16.7).

FIGURE 16.7
Set the action for your button in the Action Settings dialog box.

4. Select either **Mouse Click** or **Mouse Over** to set the action for the button (Mouse Click options require a click; Mouse Over requires only that the mouse pointer be placed on the button).

5. Choose the type of action you want to happen when the user clicks the button. Click the **Hyperlink To** drop-down list and select an action such as **Next Slide**.

6. (Optional) If you want a sound to play when the user clicks the button, select the **Play Sound** check box and choose a sound from the drop-down list.

7. Click **OK**. Your button appears on the slide.

8. View the presentation (as you learned at the beginning of this lesson) to try out the button.

If you do use buttons on your slides so that users can run the slide show, be sure you use the same style of button on each of your slides for a particular action. This kind of consistency gives the viewer of the presentation a feeling of comfort and control.

TIP

> **Buttons Can Do Many Things**   You also can create action
> buttons that run a program or fire off a macro that has
> been created using the Visual Basic for Applications pro-
> gramming language. Although these are very advanced
> features not covered in this book, keep in mind as you
> learn more about PowerPoint that many possibilities
> exist for making very creative and complex slide show
> presentations.

SETTING SLIDE SHOW OPTIONS

Depending on the type of show you're presenting, you might find it
useful to make some adjustments to the way the show runs, such as
making it run in a window (the default is full screen) or showing only
certain slides. You'll find these controls and more in the Set Up Show
dialog box, which you can open by clicking the **Slide Show** menu and
selecting **Set Up Show** (see Figure 16.8).

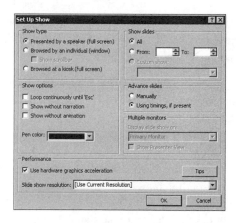

FIGURE 16.8
*Use the Set Up Show dialog box to give PowerPoint some basic instructions
about how to present your slide show.*

In this dialog box, you can choose from several options, including the following:

- Choose the medium for showing the presentation. Your choices are **Presented by a Speaker (Full Screen)**, **Browsed by an Individual (Window)**, and **Browsed at a Kiosk (Full Screen)**.

- Choose whether to loop the slide show continuously or to show it only once. You might want to loop it continuously so that it operates unaided at a kiosk at a trade show, for example.

- Show all the slides or a range of them (enter the range into the **From** and **To** boxes).

- Choose whether to advance slides manually or to use timings you set up.

- Choose a pen color. Use the Pen Color drop-down box to select a color.

In this lesson, you learned how to display a slide presentation onscreen, how to move between slides, and how to set slideshow options. You also learned to set timings and transitions for your slides and add animation schemes to the slide in the presentation. In the next lesson you learn how to print a presentation, speaker's notes, and presentation handouts.

LESSON 17

Printing Presentations, Notes, and Handouts

In this lesson, you learn how to select a size and orientation for the slides in your presentation and how to print the slides, notes, and handouts you create.

USING POWERPOINT NOTES AND HANDOUTS

Although PowerPoint presentations are designed to be shown on a computer screen, you might want to print some items related to the presentation. For example, as you design your presentation, you can enter notes related to each slide that you create in the Notes pane. These notes can then be printed out and used during the presentation.

Using speaker notes helps you keep on track during the presentation and provides you with the information that you want to present related to each slide in the presentation. When you print your notes, each slide is printed on a separate page with the notes printed below the slide.

If you want to make it easier for your presentation audience to follow the presentation and perhaps take notes of their own, you can print out handouts. Handouts provide a hard copy of each slide. The number of slides printed on each page of the handout can range from 1 to 9 slides. If you choose to print three slides per page (this is set up in the Print dialog box, which is discussed later in this lesson), PowerPoint automatically places note lines on the printout pages to the right of each slide (which makes it even easier for your audience to take notes related to the slides in the presentation).

This lesson covers the options related to printing hard copies of your slides, notes, and handouts. Let's start with a look at printing out presentation slides.

QUICK PRINTING WITH NO OPTIONS

You can quickly print all the slides in the presentation. You don't get to make any decisions about your output, but you do get your printout without delay.

To print a quick copy of each slide in the presentation, choose one of these methods:

- Click the **Print** button on the Standard toolbar.

- Choose the **File** menu, choose **Print**, and click **OK**.

- Press **Ctrl+P** and click **OK**.

The downside of printing the presentation in this way is that you will get a printout of only one slide per page in the landscape orientation. It doesn't matter what view you are in—you just get the slides. This uses up a lot of printer ink or toner, and if you want to print the presentation as an outline or print the presentation so that you can see the presentation notes that you've made, you need to access printing options that provide more control over the printout.

One way to fine-tune some of the settings that control how pages will be printed is the Page Setup dialog box.

CHANGING THE PAGE SETUP

The Page Setup dialog box enables you to select how slides, notes, and handouts should be oriented on the page (Portrait or Landscape) and the type of page that the slides should be formatted for, such as On-Screen Show, overhead sheets, or regular 8 ½-inch by 11-inch paper.

To customize the Page Setup settings, follow these steps:

1. Select the **File** menu and select **Page Setup**. The Page Setup dialog box appears as shown in Figure 17.1.

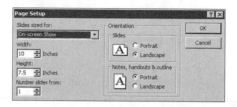

FIGURE 17.1
The Page Setup dialog box enables you to set the paper type and the orientation of slides and notes on the page.

2. Perform one of the following procedures to set the slide size:

   - To use a standard size, select a size from the **Slides Sized For** drop-down list. For example, you can have slides sized for regular 8 ½-inch by 11-inch paper, overheads, or 35mm slides (if you have a special printer that can create slides).

   - To create a custom size, enter the dimensions into the **Width** and **Height** text boxes.

TIP

> **Spin Boxes** The arrows to the right of the Width and Height text boxes enable you to adjust the settings in those boxes. Click the up arrow to increase the setting by .1 inch or the down arrow to decrease it by .1 inch.

3. In the **Number Slides From** text box, type the number with which you want to start numbering slides. (This usually is **1**, but you might want to start with a different number if the presentation is a continuation of another.)

4. Under the Slides heading, choose **Portrait** or **Landscape** orientation for your slides.

5. In the Notes, Handouts & Outline section, choose **Portrait** or
   Landscape for those items.

6. Click **OK**. If you changed the orientation of your slides, you
   might have to wait a moment while PowerPoint repositions
   the slides.

CHOOSING WHAT AND HOW TO PRINT

To really control your printouts related to a particular presentation, use
the various options supplied in the Print dialog box. The Print dialog
box enables you to specify what to print, such as handouts or the presentation as an outline; it also enables you to specify the printer to use
for the printout. For example, you might want to use a color printer
for overhead transparencies and a black-and-white printer for your
handouts. To set your print options, follow these steps:

1. Select the **File** menu and select **Print**. The Print dialog box
   appears with the name of the currently selected printer in the
   Name box (see Figure 17.2).

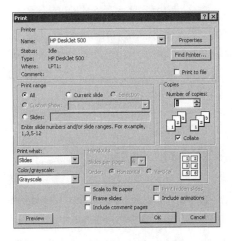

FIGURE 17.2
The Print dialog box enables you to control the printer and the printouts.

2. If you want to use a different printer, open the Name drop-down list and select the printer you want.

TIP

Printer Properties   The Properties button enables you to adjust graphics quality, select paper size, and choose which paper tray to use, among other things.

3. Choose what to print in the Print Range section:

   • Choose **All** to print all the slides in the presentation.

   • Choose **Current Slide** to print only the currently displayed slide.

   • Enter a range of slide numbers into the **Slides** text box; for example, enter **2-4** to print slides 2, 3, and 4.

4. Open the **Print What** drop-down list and choose what you want to print. You can print slides, handouts, notes, or outlines.

5. If you want more than one copy, enter the number of copies you want into the **Number of Copies** box.

6. Use the Color/Grayscale drop-down box to specify whether the printout should be in color, grayscale, or black and white.

7. If you are printing handouts, use the Handouts box on the dialog box to specify the number of slides that should be printed per page and the orientation used for the printed page (Portrait or Landscape).

8. Select or deselect any of these check boxes in the dialog box, as required:

   • **Print to File**—Select this option to send the output to a file rather than to your printer.

   • **Collate**—If you are printing more than one copy, select this check box to collate (1, 2, 3, 1, 2, 3) each printed copy instead of printing all the copies of each page at once (1, 1, 2, 2, 3, 3).

- **Scale to Fit Paper**—If the slide (or whatever you're printing) is too large to fit on the page, select this check box to decrease the size of the slide to make it fit on the page. Now you won't have to paste two pieces of paper together to see the whole slide.

- **Frame Slides**—Select this check box if you want to print a border around each slide.

- **Print Hidden Slides**—If you have any hidden slides, you can choose whether to print them. If you don't have any hidden slides, this check box will be unavailable.

- **Include Animations**—If you have any animated elements on the slide, mark this check box and Power-Point will do its best to approximate them in still form.

- **Include Comment Pages**—Prints all the comments on the slides of the presentation on a separate comments page.

TIP

> **Preview Your Printout Selection**   After specifying the various options in the Print dialog box, you might want to preview the printout before you send it to the printer. Click the **Preview** button. You are taken to the Print Preview screen. If things look good on the Print Preview screen, click **Print** to send the printout to the printer.

9. Click **OK** to print.

In this lesson, you learned how to print your presentations and how to set options in the Page Setup and Print dialog boxes. In the next lesson, you learn how to save a PowerPoint presentation for use on the World Wide Web.

LESSON 18

Designing a Presentation for the Internet

In this lesson, you'll learn how PowerPoint makes it easy to publish your presentations on the World Wide Web or your corporate intranet.

POWERPOINT AND THE WORLD WIDE WEB

The World Wide Web is the most popular and graphical component of the Internet, a worldwide network of computers. Many businesses maintain Web sites containing information about their products and services for public reading. Still other businesses maintain an internal version of the Web that's strictly for employee use, and they use the company's local area network to make it available to its staff. These are called *intranets*.

PLAIN ENGLISH

Intranet   A private corporate network that uses Internet protocols and services to share information. Intranets can use Web pages to share information among corporate intranet users.

Sooner or later, you might be asked to prepare a PowerPoint presentation for use on a Web site or an intranet. Taking a PowerPoint presentation and converting it to Web-ready content is much easier than you might think.

SPECIAL CONSIDERATIONS FOR DESIGNING WEB SHOWS

Creating a presentation for Web distribution is much like creating any other user-interactive presentation. However, consider these factors when dealing with the Web:

- For your viewers' convenience, keep the file size as small as possible. That means don't use graphics, sounds, or movies that don't serve an obvious purpose (other than providing a few additional bells and whistles in the presentation).

- Include action buttons on each slide that enable the user to jump to the previous and next slides, and possibly other action buttons, too.

- If you want the users to be able to jump from your presentation to other Web sites, be sure you include the appropriate hyperlinks. See the following section for details.

- If you convert the presentation to HTML (Web) format, anyone with a Web browser can view it on the Internet, but the presentation might not be exactly the same as the PowerPoint version of it. Depending on the Web browser used to view it, sounds, movies, transitions, and other features might not play correctly.

- If you distribute the file in PowerPoint format, your audience must have PowerPoint installed on their PCs or must download a special PowerPoint viewer (discussed later in this lesson).

ADDING URL HYPERLINKS

One way to add some Web connectivity to a PowerPoint slide presentation is by adding hyperlinks to a slide. A *hyperlink* is a link to a particular Web page, file on your computer, or even a person's e-mail address. In PowerPoint, hyperlinks can be added to a slide as text or you can create action buttons that serve as a hyperlink. For example, you might have a button that takes you to your company's home page (the top page at its Internet site) at the bottom of every slide.

PLAIN ENGLISH

> **Hyperlink**   A graphic, text entry, or button that supplies a quick link to a Web page, a file on your computer, or an e-mail address. Hyperlinks that specify URLs (Uniform Resource Locators, or Web addresses) are used to navigate from page to page on the World Wide Web.

A hyperlink can be attached to an action button (action buttons that move you from slide to slide are hyperlinks, too) or to some other graphic, or it can be attached to a string of text characters.

ASSIGNING A HYPERLINK TO AN ACTION BUTTON

The following steps show you how to assign a hyperlink to an action button:

1. Open the slide in the slide view to which you will add the hyperlink. Select the **Slide Show** menu, and then select **Action Buttons**. Select the button you wish to place on the slide from the button palette that appears. For example, use the one that looks like a house to hyperlink to your company's home page.

2. When the Action Settings dialog box appears, click the **Hyperlink To** option, button (see Figure 18.1).

3. Open the **Hyperlink To** drop-down list and select **URL**. The Hyperlink to URL dialog box appears.

FIGURE 18.1
The Action settings dialog box allows you to determine the action of the button you have created.

4. Enter the Web address in the **URL** text box (see Figure 18.2). Then click **OK**.

FIGURE 18.2
Enter the URL (the Web address) for the hyperlink.

5. Click **OK** to close the Action Settings dialog box.

If you have already created an action button and you want to change its hyperlink, select the button and select **Slide Show** then **Action Settings**. Then start at step 2 in the preceding steps to change the URL for the action button. You also can assign a hyperlink to any graphic in this same way—select the graphic and then select **Slide Show, Action Settings**. Use the Action Settings dialog box to select the hyperlink address for the graphic as listed in steps 2 through 5.

CREATING A TEXT-BASED HYPERLINK

You can insert a hyperlink on a slide as text by typing the actual URL of a site, such as **www.quehelp.com**. It will automatically be formatted as a hyperlink to the Web site. If you want to assign a hyperlink to existing text (for example, you might want to assign the www.que-help.com URL to text that says, "Que Help Site"), you need to assign the URL to the text as you assigned a URL hyperlink to an action button or image (discussed in the previous section).

To assign a hyperlink to text on a slide, follow these steps:

1. (Optional) To use existing text on a slide, select it.

2. Select the **Insert** menu, and then select **Hyperlink**. The Insert Hyperlink dialog box opens (see Figure 18.3).

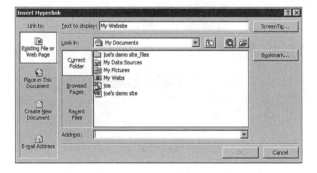

FIGURE 18.3
Use the Insert Hyperlink dialog box to assign a hyperlink to your text.

3. The text you selected in step 1 appears in the Text to Display box. If you want to change it, do so. If you didn't select any text in step 1, type the text to which you will assign the hyperlink. For example, if the URL will take them to your home page, you might type **Click here to visit my home page**.

4. If you know the address of the Web site you wish to use as the hyperlink, type the URL in the **Address** box. If you wish

to select the URL from a list of Web sites that you recently visited, click the **Browsed Pages** link in the Look In box to the left of the dialog box. Select a Web site in the list and it will appear in the Address box.

5. When you have placed a URL in the Address box, click **OK**. This will close the dialog box.

The text that you selected in step 1 or typed in step 3 will be underlined and appear in blue (typically the default color for hyperlinks). When this text is clicked on the slide during a slide show, a browser window will open displaying the Web site.

TIP

> **Auto URL Entry**   If you don't know the Web page's address, open your Web browser. Navigate to the page to which you want to link, and then jump back to PowerPoint (by clicking the PowerPoint presentation's name on the Windows taskbar). The URL is automatically entered for you in the Address box.

To test your hyperlink, view the slide in Slide Show view (discussed in Lesson 16, "Presenting an Onscreen Slide Show"), and click the button with your mouse. Your Web browser should start and the selected URL should load in it. If it doesn't work, check to be sure you entered the URL correctly. If it is correct, check your Internet connection or try again later. (Sometimes a Web page might be temporarily unavailable.)

Saving a Presentation in HTML Format

PowerPointhas the capability to save a presentation in HTML format so it can be viewed using any Web browser. PowerPoint saves in a Web format that allows your sounds, movies, animations, and other special effects to be seen just as you intended.

PLAIN ENGLISH

> **HTML**   HyperText Markup Language (HTML) is the cod-
> ing language used to build a Web page.

To save a presentation in HTML format, follow these steps:

1. Select the **File** menu, and then select **Save As Web Page**.
   The Save As dialog box appears (see Figure 18.4).

FIGURE 18.4
Choose a name for your saved Web presentation.

2. In the **File Name** text box, enter a filename for the first page
   of the presentation (the title slide). By default this is the name
   of your presentation file.

3. (Optional) If you want the page title (the name in the title bar
   when the page is displayed in a Web browser) to be different
   than the one shown, click the **Change Title** button and enter
   a different title in the Set Page Title box that appears. Click
   OK to return to the Save In dialog box.

4. Click **Save**. Your presentation is saved as an HTML file.

You might have noticed in the Save As dialog box (Figure 18.4) that there is a Publish button. This button takes you to the Publish as Web Page dialog box, in which you can set all kinds of options related to your HTML presentation, including which Web browser your audience will likely use and which slides to include. You are not required to set all these options to have your presentation saved for use on the Web.

A saved HTML presentation actually consists of several files, not just a single HTML file. PowerPoint creates a home page (an entry point) with the same name as the original presentation. (This is the file you were naming when you chose a name in step 2.) For example, if the presentation file was named Broadway.ppt, the home page would be named Broadway.htm.

A folder is also created for the HTML presentation, which is given the name of the presentation (for example, Broadway Files). This folder contains all the other HTML, graphics, and other files needed to display the complete presentation. If you are transferring the HTML presentation to another PC (which is very likely, if you are going to make it available on the Internet through a Web server), you must transfer not only the lone HTML home page but also the entire associated folder.

VIEWING YOUR WEB PRESENTATION

As you work on a slide presentation that you plan on making part of a Web page (and have it viewed online), you can preview your presentation in Internet Explorer (or any compatible Web browser) to see how the slides look and operate as Web content. Viewing the presentation in Internet Explorer can really help you fine-tune the presentation for the Web before you actually make it available to your audience.

To view your current presentation in Internet Explorer (or your default Web browser), follow these steps:

1. Select the **File** menu, and then choose **Web Page Preview**. The Internet Explorer Window will appear showing the first slide in your presentation (see Figure 18.5).

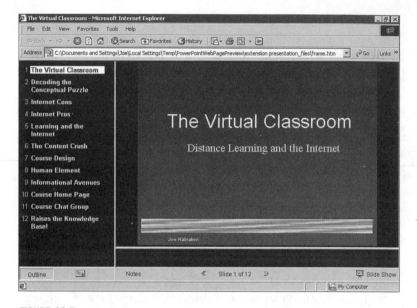

FIGURE 18.5
You can preview your presentation for the Web.

2. Use the navigation pane (on the left side of the Explorer window) to view each slide in the presentation. You also can navigate the presentation using the navigation buttons found below the main slide pane.

3. When you have finished previewing the presentation in Internet Explorer, click the Explorer **Close** button.

When you close the Internet Explorer window, you will be returned to the PowerPoint window. You can now fine-tune the presentation for the Web and preview it as needed.

In this lesson, you learned about PowerPoint's capabilities in helping you present your slides on the Web.

INDEX

R

S

W

X–Y–Z